Physical Characteristics of the Skye Terrier

(from the American Kennel Club breed standard)

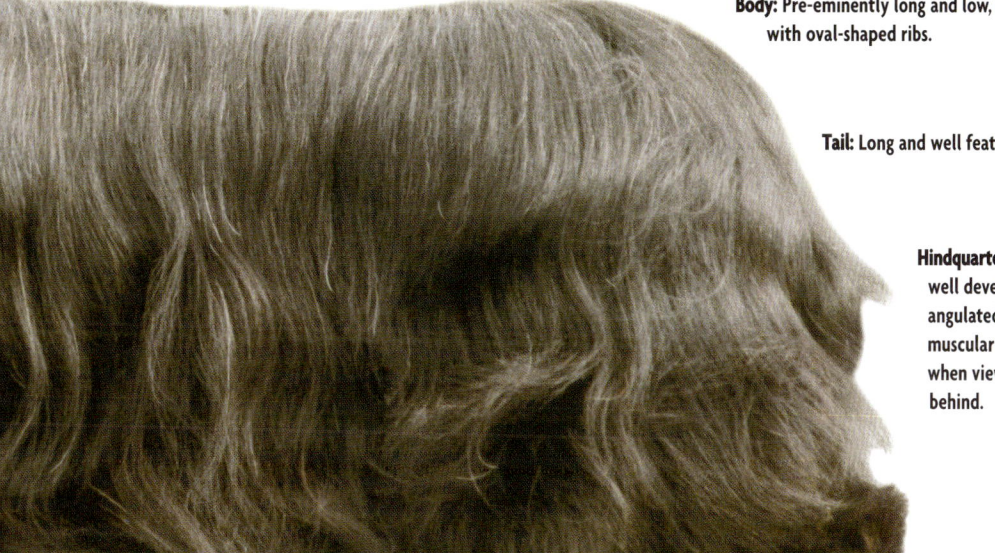

Backline: Level.

Body: Pre-eminently long and low, the chest deep, with oval-shaped ribs.

Tail: Long and well feathered.

Hindquarters: Strong, full, well developed and well angulated. Legs short, muscular and straight when viewed from behind.

Feet: Large hare-feet preferably pointing forward.

Size: Ideal shoulder height for dogs is 10 inches and bitches 9.5 inches.

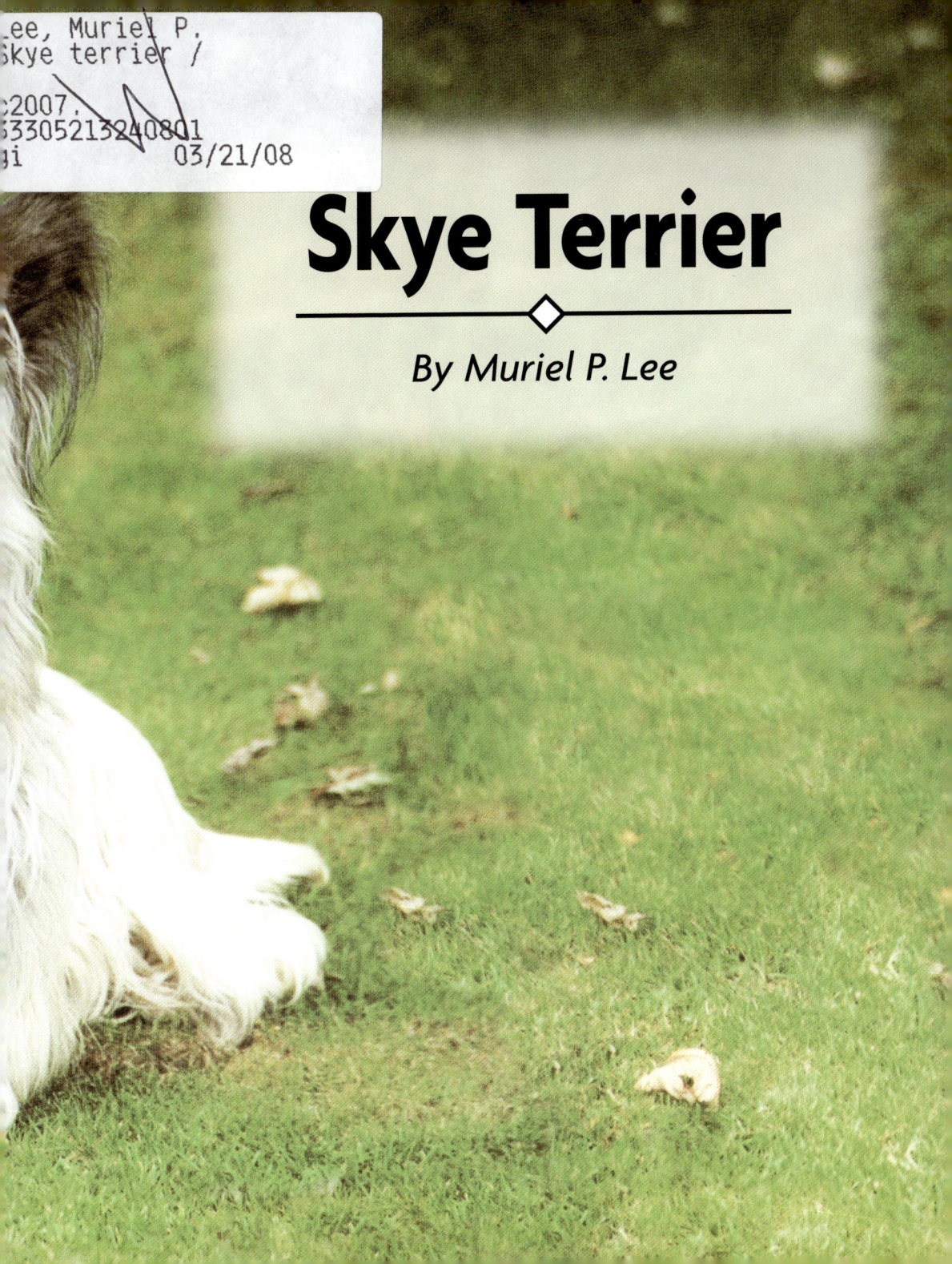

Skye Terrier

By Muriel P. Lee

9   History of the Skye Terrier

Meet the rugged terrier hailing from the Isle of Skye. A familiar face in his native Great Britain, see how this charming lad won hearts the world over to gain him a band of fanciers with unmatched devotion to their breed. Meet influential dogs and breeders, and read the enchanting story of perhaps the most famous Skye, Greyfriar's Bobby.

22   Characteristics of the Skye Terrier

The Skye's body type and coat set him apart in looks from his terrier brethren, but make no mistake—he is all terrier in spirit. Intelligence, independence, courage and a zest for life are at the fore of the Skye's temperament; are you up for the challenge? The breed's physical characteristics, personality, owner suitability and hereditary health concerns are among topics discussed.

26   Breed Standard for the Skye Terrier

Learn the requirements of a well-bred Skye Terrier by studying the description of the breed set forth in the American Kennel Club standard. Both show dogs and pets must possess key characteristics as outlined in the breed standard.

30   Your Puppy Skye Terrier

Find out about how to locate a well-bred Skye Terrier puppy. Discover which questions to ask the breeder and what to expect when visiting the litter. Prepare for your puppy-accessory shopping spree. Also discussed are home safety, the first trip to the vet, socialization and solving basic puppy problems.

52   Proper Care of Your Skye Terrier

Cover the specifics of taking care of your Skye Terrier every day: feeding for the puppy, adult and senior dog; grooming, including coat care, ears, eyes, nails and bathing; and exercise needs for your dog. Also discussed are the essentials of dog identification.

70   Training Your Skye Terrier

Begin with the basics of training the puppy and adult dog. Learn the principles of housetraining the Skye Terrier, including the use of crates and basic scent instincts. Get started by introducing the pup to his collar and leash and progress to the basic commands. Find out about obedience classes and other activities.

Contents

Healthcare of Your Skye Terrier 93

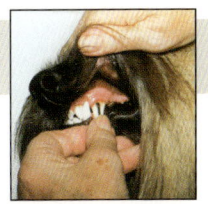

By Lowell Ackerman DVM, DACVD
Become your dog's healthcare advocate and a well-educated canine keeper. Select a skilled and able veterinarian. Discuss pet insurance, vaccinations and infectious diseases, the neuter/spay decision and a sensible, effective plan for parasite control, including fleas, ticks and worms.

Your Senior Skye Terrier 121

Know when to consider your Skye Terrier a senior and what special needs he will have. Learn to recognize the signs of aging in terms of physical and behavioral traits and what your vet can do to optimize your dog's golden years. Consider some advice about saying goodbye to your beloved pet.

Showing Your Skye Terrier 127

Step into the center ring and find out about the world of showing pure-bred dogs. Here's how to get started in AKC shows, how they are organized and what's required for your dog to become a champion. Take a leap into the realms of obedience trials, agility, earthdog events and tracking tests.

Behavior of Your Skye Terrier 141

Analyze the canine mind to understand what makes your Skye Terrier tick. The following potential problems are addressed: aggression (fear-biting, inter-canine and dominant), separation anxiety, sexual misconduct, chewing, digging, jumping up, barking and food-related problems.

Index........ 156

KENNEL CLUB BOOKS® SKYE TERRIER
ISBN: 1-59378-302-7

Copyright © 2007 • Kennel Club Books, LLC • 308 Main Street, Allenhurst, NJ 07711 USA
Cover Design Patented: US 6,435,559 B2 • Printed in South Korea

All rights reserved. No part of this book may be reproduced in any form, by photostat, scanner, microfilm, xerography or any other means, or incorporated into any information retrieval system, electronic or mechanical, without the written permission of the copyright owner.

Library of Congress Cataloging-in-Publication Data
Lee, Muriel P.
  Skye terrier / by Muriel P. Lee.
    p. cm.
  ISBN 1-59378-302-7
  1. Skye terriers. I. Title.
  SF429.S67L44 2006
  636.755—dc22   2006012319

10 9 8 7 6 5 4 3 2 1

Photography by Carol Ann Johnson and Alice van Kempen
with additional photographs by:

John Ashbey, Kim Booth, Paulette Braun, Bushman Photography, Alan and Sandy Carey, Carolina Biological Supply, DAG, Downey Dog Show Photography, Laurie J. Erickson, Isabelle Français, Bill Jonas, Dr. Dennis Kunkel, Tam C. Nguyen, Don Petrulis, Phototake, Jean Claude Revy and Alice Roche.

Illustrations by Patricia Peters.

The publisher wishes to thank all of the owners whose dogs are illustrated in this book, including Mr. Lankhaar, Mrs. Sue McCourt, Ms. Laura Weber and Mrs. Welkenhuyzen.

SKYE TERRIER

From Vero Shaw's famous *Book of the Dog*, published in 1881, comes this lovely drawing of early Skye Terriers, exhibiting both the drop and prick ears. The two ear carriages have been a part of the breed's history since the breed's inception.

HISTORY OF THE
SKYE TERRIER

It is thought that the modern Skye Terrier evolved in the late 16th century on the Isle of Skye, one of the rugged Hebrides islands of northwestern Scotland. From that time to the late 19th century, refinements continued to be made in the breed. Early references are made to Lady MacDonald and her dogs at Armadale Castle in Sleat, located at the southern tip of Skye. Some theorize that this breed was a cross of native Scottish terriers with some Spanish white dogs, possibly of Maltese origins, which survived the shipwrecks of the Spanish Armada. Through the centuries, not only were the Skye Terriers tireless workers in the field but they provided their owners with companionship and loyalty.

THE SKYE IN BRITAIN
By 1826, Skyes were found in abundance on the Isle of Skye as well as on the Isles of Wight and Mull. In 1842, Queen Victoria received her first Skye and, with Her Majesty's blessing, the breed became popular. Before long, the Skye Terrier was a familiar dog throughout Scotland and England.

SKYE TERRIER

> **GREYFRIAR'S BOBBY**
>
> Sometime in the mid-1800s, John Gray acquired a Skye Terrier through his work as a police officer. Gray, accompanied by his shaggy dog, Bobby, went to market every Wednesday and when the castle cannon boomed at 1 P.M., Gray and his dog went to the local coffee house for lunch, a block from Greyfriar's churchyard. Gray had his lunch, and Bobby had a bun followed by a bone.
>
> Gray died in 1858 and was buried in the Greyfriar's cemetery. The little dog visited the restaurant every day when he heard the cannon. He would be given his bun and bone, and, after eating, he retraced his steps to the cemetery to sleep on his master's grave. He did this for 14 years until his death of old age. After his death, a memorial fountain was erected on the corner by the churchyard gate. Of course, the shaggy dog was a Skye Terrier, and the fountain can be seen whenever you travel to Edinburgh.

An illustration of Greyfriar's Bobby at the tomb of his master from the picture by Gourley Steele, originally published in 1924.

The breed appeared in many paintings by well-known artists and became a common sight at the dog shows. During this time, the drop-eared variety was much more popular than the erect-, or prick-, eared Skye. From 1890 on, the judges preferred the erect ears, but there remained two separate classes for the two varieties at the dog shows.

The most famous Skye kennel by the turn of the 19th century was Mrs. W. J. Hughes's Wolverley kennels. Her dogs, Wolverley Roy, Wolverley Jock and Wolverley Duchess, were all big winners in their day. Mrs. Hughes was presented by command to the Princess of Wales, later Queen Alexandria, in recognition of being the owner of the most perfect kennel of Skyes in England. Eng. Ch. Wolverley Chummie, considered the best Skye of all time and owned by Miss McCheane, won 31 championships, sired 14 champions and was never beaten in the ring.

By the early 1900s, entries for the Skye could be as high as 110 in a show. However, when World War I broke out, just owning a dog became very difficult. After the war, when breeding was again possible, some historians believe that the long, thick coat and its upkeep became a factor for the breed's suffering a decline. By 1920, registrations had dropped so low that classes for the two vari-

History

Artists and naturalists have long been fascinated with the creatures of the Isle of Skye. From the 1840 book *Dogs from Naturalist's Library* comes this illustration entitled "Isle of Skye Terrier."

eties (the drop-eared and prick-eared) were combined and all Skye Terriers were shown under one classification, regardless of ear type.

Between the two World Wars, Merrymount kennels, established in 1906, came to the fore. Merrymount kennels of Lady Marcia Miles was founded on the famous Wolverley dogs. Lady Miles's mother, Hon. Mrs. Jocelyn, also had a large kennel of Skyes, so Lady Miles had been well familiar with the breed all her life. At the age of eight, she saw a team of Wolverley Skyes at a show and so greatly admired their full coats and grooming that she vowed that one day she would have a kennel of Skyes to match the Wolverleys's.

Over 100 champions came out of the Merrymount kennels. Among the greats were Eng./Am. Ch. Royalist of Merrymount, exported to the United States to the Iradell kennels; Eng./Am. Ch. Merrymount You'll Do, also exported to America to the Iradell kennels ("of Iradell" was then added to the end of the dog's name); and Eng. Ch. Merrymount Sunset, an outstanding brood bitch who had several drop-eared progeny. Mrs. Miles's death in 1972 was a great loss to the whole dog fancy.

Marion von Feldmahr Crook, born in Vienna but living in Great Britain with her British husband, moved to the village of Rhosneigr on the west coast of Anglesey, North Wales, where they founded the well-known Rhosneigr kennels. Many outstanding champions were produced by this kennel, including Eng. Ch. Rhosneigr Red Shoes, who was Best of Breed at the Crufts Dog Show in 1959 and 1960 and then exported to America to the Merrybrac kennels, and Eng. Ch. Rhosneigr Rising Star, another winner who was exported to the United States to the Iradell kennels. Rhosneigr kennels thrived for many decades and was still active in the 1990s.

The most important Skye Terrier in the early days of the breed, bred by Mrs. Hughes, was Eng. Ch. Wolverley Chummie, who won an inordinate number of honors in his day.

Eng. Ch. Diana, bred by Mrs. L. King, was born in 1924 and won her first Challenge Certificate in 1928.

Eng. Ch. Luckie Henry, bred by Miss Watson in 1926, won three Challenge Certificates in 1930 to become a champion.

Brigitte Helm, the famous German film star of the 1930s, with her best friend, a prick-eared Skye Terrier.

From the end of World War II and through the 1960s, many English kennels deserve mention not only because of the quality of the dogs they produced but also because of the winners that they had in the show ring. The Meerend kennels of Mrs. Cuthbert and her daughter Miss Manville was active for over 30 years. Mrs. Harold Eaden's "of Mynd" kennels owned and bred some notable bitches, as did the Faygate kennels of Miss Alexander.

SKYES IN THE UNITED STATES
The first Skye Terrier registered in the United States was Romach, whelped in England in 1884 and registered in 1887 to Malzeland kennels in Duchess County, New York. The Skye was not a particularly popular breed in America, but there were a few early supporters and exhibitors. William Sanderson of Philadelphia exhibited Skyes that were consistent winners in the late 1800s. There were several other exhibitors of Skyes prior to 1900, all situated in the East. George William Donaldson, from Philadelphia as

> **STONEHENGE ON SKYES**
> Dr. J. Caius, in 1576, wrote in *Englishe Dogges* about the Skye Terrier, "A beggarly beast brought out of the barbarous borders from the uttermost contryes northward."

well, was successful in the show ring, and his niece noted that he was truly the first American breeder/exhibitor of Skyes, as the other exhibitors were showing stock bred in and imported from Europe. Mr. Donaldson sent several Skyes to his sister in San Francisco, so the breed was seen on the West Coast as early as 1900.

Even though the Skye was not a particularly popular breed, the entries at the shows in the late 1800s reached as high as 50 or 60 dogs. Pittsburgh, Philadelphia, Boston, New York and Washington DC were the primary areas where there were Skye entries at dog shows.

For whatever reason, the popularity of the breed dropped after 1900, and by 1905 there were no Skye entries at the Westminster Kennel Club show. A few Skyes were shown in the following year, but from 1913 to 1927 there were no entries at Westminster.

In 1927 Michael Stillman, of Roseland, New Jersey, imported a bitch from England for his wife. She was bred to a stud that had been imported from Sweden and thus began the Arreton kennels of the Stillmans. The Stillmans were active in the breed for many years with their best known dog being Ch. Scottish Chief of Arreton, a Best in Show winner. The Stillmans produced exceptional Skyes over their many years in the breed.

ASHES TO ASHES
After his death in 1891, the remains of Eng. Ch. Wolverley Chummie were donated to the National History Museum in Cromwell and were on exhibit there until the building was bombed and nearly destroyed in World War II.

In the mid-1930s Mrs. N. Clarkson Earl, Jr. from Connecticut discovered Skye Terriers while vacationing in France. Unfortunately, the two French puppies she purchased died from distemper on the trip back to the US, but Mrs. Earl was not to be deterred and purchased two Skye puppies from Mrs. Stillman. By 1937 Mrs. Earl had two brood bitches, and this was the beginning of the very well-known Iradell kennels. Mrs. Earl wrote, "I called Mrs. Stillman and asked her what she had for sale. I will never forget her arrival at my New York house one wintry afternoon in 1935 bringing two desperately cunning looking four-month-old 'Mickey Mouse' bundles of fur peering out at me from a basket. I bought them without further ado."

Mrs. Earl was active in the breed for the next 30 years, breeding over 50 Skye Terrier champions. Ch. Bracadale Henry was Best of Breed at Westminster from 1938 through 1943 and also won the Breed at the prestigious Morris and Essex show from 1938 to 1941. This Skye was second in the Terrier Group at Westminster in 1942, and in 1953 her import Eng./Am. Ch. Merrymount You'll Do Of Iradell won the Group there as well.

In the mid-1940s, Ch. Bracadale Tiggy of Iradell was the first Skye to win an all-breed Best in Show in America. Ch. Ivory Jock of Iradell won 11 all-breed Bests in Show, and in 1956 he was the top terrier and in the top 12 show dogs all breeds. Later, Ch. Toby of Iradell was another multiple Best in Show dog for the kennel.

> **AN HIGHLAND WARRIOR**
> Famed author Robert Louis Stevenson had a Skye named Wattie. He wrote, "Wattie was the king in the Stevenson home for six years and battled birds and cats of the neighborhood. He rose, stiff with wrath, if any alien foot profaned the path." The dog eventually was killed in a fight with a larger dog. Stevenson wrote, "He died like an Highland warrior. Poor wee man, he died in a fight, which is what he would have chosen, for military glory was more in his line than domestic virtue."

The famed American soprano and movie star Jeanette MacDonald with her Skye named Stormy Weather. Often photographed with her dog, Miss MacDonald was instrumental in popularizing the breed in the US.

The Skye Terrier Club of America (STCA), under the leadership of Mrs. Earl, was founded in January 1938. There were 18 founding members, including Mrs. Adele Goodman of the famous Glamoor kennels. Mrs. Earl served over 15 years as president of the club.

Another well-known breeder from the 1930s was Mrs. Charles S. Dewey, Jr. of High Times kennels. As with other breeders of the times, top stock was purchased from England and France as well as stock from Mrs. Stillman of the Arreton kennels. Ch. High Times Gesture of Arreton was dam of the Best in Show-winning Ch. High Times Miss Gesty, owned by Adele Goodman.

At the end of the 1930s the Merrybrac kennels, owned by Mrs. Eben W. Pyne of Long Island, was started with an English import. An exceptional dog from this kennel was Ch. Merrybrac's Mustang, Best of Breed at Morris and Essex and winner of three STCA specialty shows. Mrs. Pyne remained an active fancier in the breed for many years, even after she was no longer breeding her excellent Skyes.

During the years of World War II, the breeding of dogs was greatly curtailed in the US as it was in Europe. However, Ch. Bracadale Henry placed second in the Terrier Group at Westminster in 1943. Not long after, activity started to pick up in both America and Britain. It wasn't long before British and French Skyes were once again being imported into the US.

The Stonebrae kennels of Mrs. W. H. Tompkins owned Ch. Little Cap of Stonebrae, the first of the Skye Terriers to win multiple Bests

A successful day for Am./Can. Ch. Sand Island Sam Fifield TD.

Ch. Dunvegan Tail Toddle, shown winning Best of Breed under judge Amy Stevenson in 1976.

SKYE TERRIER

Ch. Sand Island Soltaire, a top winner from the mid-1980s.

in Show and a Quaker Oats Award winner in 1953 for Best Terrier. In addition he won nearly 60 Group firsts and numerous Group placements. By now, the Skye Terrier was surely becoming a formidable competitor in the Group ring.

In 1935 a mother and son duo became active in the breed and were to remain lifelong breeders, fanciers and lovers of the Skye Terrier. Mrs. Adele Goodman and her son Walter imported two Skyes from England, which they were urged to show. In time they purchased Ch. High Times Miss Gesty. With Walter grooming and handling, Miss Gesty became the first American-bred Skye to win an all-breed Best in Show award. Thereafter the wins from this kennel of outstanding Skyes were the talk of the town, and they were tough competition in any Group or Best in Show line up.

The Goodman's first homebred Skye, a son of Miss Gesty, was Am./Fr./Int. Ch. Glamoor Going Up, 18-time Group winner and a Best in Show dog. In the late 1950s the Goodmans imported the cream bitch Ch. Evening Star de Luchar from France. She went on to win over 70 Terrier Groups and 21 Bests in Show. As usual, all dogs were owner-handled by Walter Goodman. A later import from France, Ch. Jacinthe de Ricelaine won nearly 100 Terrier Groups and 36 Bests in Show. She was in the Terrier Group's top ten five times and a top all-breed dog. In addition to the illustrious show career, she whelped a litter of nine, all of which became champions and included Best in Show winners Ch. Glamoor Good News, the victor at Westminster in 1969, and Ch. Glamoor Go Go Go. Other big winners for the Glamoor

> **DROP AND PRICK EARS**
> Until around 1890, most of the Skye Terriers were of the drop-eared variety, but, after that, the prick ear became more popular. In the drop-eared variety, the ears hang flat and against the skull and, of course, the prick ears are held erect with the hair flowing over the top of the ears and down on the dog's face. Both types of ears are acceptable for showing in England and the United States, but, in both countries, the prick ear is by far the more popular.

kennels, in addition to Go Go Go, who was the winner of numerous Bests in Show and Terrier Groups, was Ch. Glamoor Gang Buster, the fifth generation of Glamoor breeding. On trips to Europe the dogs were taken along and several of them gained international titles as well.

The Glamoor kennels were active for many decades and made a huge impact on the Skye Terrier breed. Although Mrs. Goodman passed away some years ago, Walter Goodman is still very active in dogs and president of the Montgomery County Kennel Club, which hosts the very prestigious all-terrier show in the US. In addition, he is the delegate to the American Kennel Club from the Skye Terrier Club of America.

Many individuals who had a love for the Skye Terrier became active during the 1960s. Druidmoor kennels of Charles Brown, Jr., in Beverly Hills, imported several dogs from France from the renowned kennels of Madame Chamart. He also imported a male from Holland, Dutch/Bel./Int. Ch. Jimmy de Ricelaine, litter brother to Walter Goodman's Ch. Jacinthe de Ricelaine. Many nice wins came from this kennel of limited breeding.

A small kennel of the 1960s and 1970s was Edrie Weehunt's Cimarron kennels, located in Oklahoma. Ch. Cimarron Sarason Andrew won several Groups and a Best in Show and was the number-two Skye Terrier in 1970, 1971 and 1972.

The Gleanntan kennels of B. Nolan and Donna Dale in Maryland started in the late 1960s.

Winning Best in Show at the Chicago Goldcoast Kennel Club in 2000, Ch. Gleanntan Gee Whillikers with judge Dr. Robert Indeglia.

THE SKYE TERRIERS AND HUNTING

The Skyes would run with the hounds and when the hounds chased the prey, often otters, fox and other field vermin, into the cairns (heaps of stones), the Skyes, with their long and low bodies, would wriggle through the stones and drive the prey out for the hunters to kill. The heavy coat on the Skye provided protection, and his particular body conformation allowed him to enter spaces that few other dogs could enter. His courage, stamina and endurance were legendary.

Their foundation bitch, Ch. Jojac's Rise and Shine was bred to Ch. Glamoor Gang Buster and from this litter came the top-producing bitch Ch. Gleanntan Coming At Ya, a multiple Best in Specialty Show bitch and a producer of nine champions. She was the top-producing dam, all breeds, in 1972. Donna was very active in the breed, in the STCA and as a mentor to many. The kennel has produced nearly 100 champions, including all breed Best in Show winners. Unfortunately, Donna passed away in 2001.

Olga Smid of Olivia kennels came to the US from Czechoslovakia in 1968. She has produced many American champion Skyes in addition to Skye champions throughout the world. She is still active in the breed and judges all Terriers and some Non-Sporting and Toy breeds.

Mrs. J. Jay Amann from Oklahoma was also active in the 1960s and 1970s with her Quizas kennels. Ch. Quetzan Brucie O'Duff (kennel name was later changed to Quizas) was a multi-Group winner in the US and Mexico and sired 14 champions. His son, Ch. Quizas Casey O'Bruce won Terrier Groups in the US, Mexico and South America and was Best of Breed at Westminster in 1971. Over 30 champions have come out of this kennel.

Roblyn kennels of Bob and Anne Boucher in Minnesota bred a number of champions over the years and were great supporters of the breed. Ch. Roblyn's Racy Rachel, bred to Ch. Glamoor Gang Buster, produced Ch. Roblyn's Bhain Inghean, winner of several Terrier Groups and sire of six champions. Ch. Roblyn's Hotter Than That was a Best in Show and multiple-Group winner. Anne was active in the breed and in the STCA, in addition to being a Terrier Group judge, until the time of her death in 2005.

Carol Simonds and her daughter Janice of Rover Run kennels in California have been active since 1965. Their first Skye, Ch. Wishau of Iradell, won many Group placements. Ch. Rover Run The California Zephyr, owned and bred by Carol and Jan and co-owned with Don and Anne Brown, had multiple-Group placements. They have bred many Skye Terrier champions and in recent years have also become involved with the Sealyham Terrier.

Many breeders are coming along to continue the work of the dedicated breeders who have gone on before them. Laura Weber of Lairdoglen kennels in Minnesota started with the Roblyn line and is breeding excellent dogs. In addition, Laura is active in the STCA and also with performance Skyes. Her homebred Ch.

History

Lairdoglen Braveheart, owned by Michel Koss, Gail Smith and Tim and Diane Brown, is a multi-group-winning Skye.

Michael Pesare, teamed up with B. Nolan Dale and Roxanna Rohrich, is carrying on the Gleanntan name and traditions. Ch. Gleanntan Gotitxactlyrite, handled by Michael, was the number-one Skye in 2003 and a Pedigree Award winner. Ch. Gleanntan Grandxpose was the number-one Skye bitch for 2001 and 2002. Ch. Gleanntan Gee Whillikers was the number-one Skye in 2000, winning eight all-breed Bests in Show, Bests in Specialty Show and a Pedigree Award.

The Skye Terrier's history is long and glorious and its supporters are numerous. The breed will always be beloved in the United States.

SKYES ON THE CONTINENT

Skye Terriers are known and are popular throughout the world. It was thought that the mother of Marie Antoinette owned the first Skye in Austria. Frau Janisch was a great Austrian Skye fancier and her English import, Crown Prince Charles of Meerend, won his world championship at the World Dog Show in Frankfurt in 1935. Herr Steinbacher's Austrian kennel imported several dogs from Talisker kennels.

Skyes have been popular in Germany since the early 1900s. Crown Princess Cecilia and Princess Pless showed their Skyes in the 1930s. Frau Dillis had an impressive kennel in the 1960s and imported several dogs from the Isle of Skye and the former Czechoslovakia. In 1973 Gloriette v Muencher Kindl won her world championship title, and in 1976 at

Ch. Quizas Casey O'Bruce, owner-handled by Jay Amann under judge Forrest Hall in 1971, was one of the top-winning Skye Terriers for several years in the early 1970s.

Not only does Ch. Roblyn A Chorus Line present well in the show ring, this dog earned a Tracking Dog Excellent title!

Here's Am./Can. Ch. Lairdoglen Renaisance Man winning a Best of Opposite award at the Lake Minnetonka Kennel Club in 2000.

the World Dog Show in Innsbruck, she won the world championship title again under breeder-judge Olga Smid. The Morningsky kennels of Elke Spinnrock are well known, with Int./World Ch. Alpha of Morningsky's having won the world championship in 1978 and 1981. This dog is behind most of the top winners in many countries today. The kennel is known for outstanding blacks.

In Belgium, Italy, France, Switzerland and the Netherlands, there are many Skye fanciers. In addition, the former Czechoslovakia, the former Yugoslavia, Poland and Russia all have breeders of quality.

In the Scandinavian countries, the Skye was imported as early as 1883. In Denmark, by the 1920s, a number of Swedish dogs were imported and the breed continued its popularity. The breed has had difficulty in achieving success in Norway, but in the 1980s a number of Skyes were imported from Sweden. However, at this time, the breed has only a small following in the country. Sweden has its loyal supporters and breeders: Mr. and Mrs. Swensen and their Skylab kennels, with foundation from Skyeline kennels in Finland, have achieved great success in the breed. They purchased Opulous of Skyeline, and he achieved an outstanding show record in addition to being an exceptional sire. Through the 1980s and 1990s, many breeders were active in the breed and produced some lovely Skyes.

Mrs. Hjordis Westerholm of Finland has been a very active breeder under the Skyeline prefix. She bred numerous Finnish champions before retiring to England in the 1980s. Finnsky kennels has also produced outstanding dogs in addition to importing excellent specimens from Sweden and Switzerland. Other kennel names of note are the Tuukan kennels and the Skyroyal kennels. The Finnish have been very active in the breed, with over 300 members in the Finnish Skye Terrier Club. The club is active in holding matches, lectures and camps and in encouraging newcomers to the breed.

Although the Skye is known throughout the world, the breed has not been forgotten on its island of origin. The Isle of Skye kennels of Lia Obee produced some outstanding dogs in the 1980s and 1990s. Her exceptional cream

History

Finnish-bred Skye Terriers have done well at Westminster, winning numerous Bests of Breed and Group firsts. In 2003 the breed winner was Ch. Albatross of Skyeline, shown by Eugene Zaphiris under judge Karen Wilson.

bitch, Ch. Cimarron Czigana v d Litsberg, was bred to Int. Ch. Olivia Wild West and produced the "Winter" dogs: Winter Wish, Winter Wheat, Winter Witch and Winter Whisper, all champions, with Whisper becoming a multi-national champion who won several Groups in the Netherlands and Denmark in 1986. Cimmaron was then bred to her son, Whisper, and out of this litter Brilliant Brisk of the Isle of Skye became one of the top-winning Skyes in the Netherlands. Int. Ch. x Littlecreek Reay was added to the kennel, and she has become an impressive brood bitch in addition to her impressive number of titles.

The little dog who had its start on the farms of the rugged country of the Isle of Skye has surely come a long way in 150 years. Hail the Skye!

CHARACTERISTICS OF THE SKYE TERRIER

Some terriers, like the Skye, are "below the knee" in size. Unlike his fellow Scottish brethren, the West Highland White Terrier, the Cairn Terrier and the Scottish Terrier, who are rather boxy in shape, the Skye Terrier has a long body and is basically twice as long as he is high. In addition, rather than a fairly short, harsh coat that fits like a jacket, he has a long, flowing coat that is brushed and never stripped.

Will Judy wrote about the Skye in 1936, "The pricked ear dog suggests a Papillon...and when the ears are pendant or hanging, it is difficult for the judge to tell which end of the dog means action and this he may discover too late. The Skye is a doormat that has four feet to carry it." A delightful, insightful, if somewhat unkind, description of this magnificent breed only makes fanciers more fascinated with the Skye Terrier. Although the Cairn, Westie and Scottie are somewhat similar in characteristics, the Skye is similar to the Dandie Dinmont with his low-slung body but does not carry the roached topline of the Dandie.

The English standard for the Skye notes that this breed is elegant and dignified, and the American standard notes that he is a dog of style, elegance and dignity. The American standard also mentions that he has sturdy bone and hard muscle and is strong in body, solidly built, full of strength and with substantial bone. He has a long and powerful head, short and muscular legs and large feet. Note that this is a good-sized, masculine dog who will do a day's work if needed, but who will also join you on the sofa for an evening of relaxation.

THE INDEPENDENT SKYE
Common characteristics for all terriers are their desire to work with great enthusiasm and courage. They all have large and powerful teeth for their size, and they have keen hearing and excellent eyesight. No matter how many generations for which they have been pets, the hunting/going-to-ground purpose for which the breed was bred will remain with the dog. The Skye is a terrier through and through. His Scottish background shows in his rather

staid, reserved and dignified mien, as well as what can be a streak of stubbornness. He has a mind of his own and does not suffer fools lightly.

The Skye is not a good dog for a first-time dog owner. Better to start with a retriever or Border Collie, dogs that like to please their masters. All of the terriers are bright, quick and independent. With minds of their own, they are not always easily trained and will take the upper hand in a household as soon as they sense (rightly or not) that their owner does not know what he is doing. Skyes are independent thinkers, confident and intelligent, but should never be shy or mean.

Counted among the most handsome of terriers, the Skye is an eye-catching, heart-warming pure-bred choice.

However, this being said, if you are looking for one of the handsomest of terriers, one who will be a smart companion, not only in brains but in looks, and if you enjoy a challenge, you will love the Skye! Prolific pet-book author Andrew De Prisco, in his book *Choosing a Dog for Life*, sums the breed up: "As his fanciers will acclaim, as terriers go, the Skye's the limit!"

Like the Scottish Terrier, he is also sensitive and does not respond well to harsh discipline. He must be persuaded to obey, and if not given firm and intelligent training, with love, he can grow up to become a difficult adult dog. Given a good home life, the Skye Terrier will become a loyal and loving family companion.

If you are a first-time dog owner, you must be aware of your responsibility toward your new

HEART-HEALTHY

In this modern age of ever-improving cardio-care, no doctor or scientist can dispute the advantages of owning a dog to lower a person's risk of heart disease. Studies have proven that petting a dog, walking a dog and grooming a dog all show positive results toward lowering your blood pressure. The simple routine of exercising your dog—going outside with the dog and walking, jogging or playing catch—is heart-healthy in and of itself. If you are normally less active than your physician thinks you should be, adopting a dog may be a smart option to improve your own quality of life as well as that of another creature.

These two talented Skye Terriers are contemplating what their next competitive pursuit will be. Sometimes quiet time on the sofa is all a Skye needs at that given moment.

friend. You must either keep your dog on a leash or in your securely fenced yard. Your Skye, if loose and trotting along at your side, will spot a squirrel across a busy street and his instinct will be to react quickly. He will dart across the street, never minding the traffic. Therefore, some rudimentary obedience training should be undertaken so that your chum will sit when asked to, come when called and, in general, act like a little gentleman.

Skyes, as with other terriers, can be a challenge in the obedience ring. Terriers are not easy dogs to work with in obedience. In training, their keen intelligence and independent spirit can sometimes be more trying than owners anticipate. You will see Golden Retrievers, Poodles and Border Collies in abundance excelling in obedience classes, as these are breeds that are easy to work with. Not only are they intelligent but, more importantly, they have a willingness to please their masters. Obedience classes with your Skye Terrier should be seriously considered for your sake and for that of the dog. Six sessions of obedience will at least teach you and your dog the rudiments of stay, come, sit and heel. The terrier is easily distracted and busy, but he is an intelligent dog and he can respond to training. Of course, when training a smart and independent dog, the handler will often learn humility while the dog is learning his sits and stays.

HEREDITARY CONCERNS IN THE SKYE

Do be aware when purchasing the Skye Terrier that there are some issues in the breed that you may not encounter in other breeds. First of all, this is a breed that needs to be thoroughly groomed on a weekly basis and touched up as necessary. Secondly, as with all other breeds of dog, there are some health and genetic problems of which you should be aware.

Breast cancer is the primary problem in the breed. Watch for abnormal swellings around the breasts and lymph nodes. Watch for loss of appetite, weight loss and any discharges. If you notice a lump, take your dog to the veterinarian where a biopsy of the tumor will be taken to determine if it is cancerous. Treatment options should be discussed with your vet, always keeping in mind the well-being of your dog as well as the age. If you opt for surgical treatment, ask what the outcome is expected to be, and you may want to check into the cost of the surgery.

Hermangiosarcoma is the second most common cause of death in the Skye. This is a splenic tumor that can rupture before it is diagnosed. The spleen is an immunologic filter of the blood, containing many important cells of the immune system. Treatment is early diagnosis and removal of the tumor before it has a chance to spread.

Auto-immune disease is also present in the breed, affecting Skyes between the ages of three to six years. Another immune problem seen in the breed is hypothyroidism, which manifests as dry coat and skin allergies. Diagnosis through a blood test is easy, and treatment with thyroid supplements is very effective.

Disk disease is found in 10% of the breed, as well as puppy limp or Skye limp. This is a painful limp that can be caused by a premature closure of the distal radial growth plate.

Hypertrophic osteodystrophy also affects Skyes. This is caused by rapidly growing long bones, which appear to outgrow the blood supply. All of these are problems that must be diagnosed and discussed with either your vet or with a specialist at a university's veterinary school.

As daunting as this list may seem, the Skye Terrier is really a very hardy breed, as most terriers are. The problems mentioned exist in the breed and a puppy buyer should be aware of them. These diseases are very uncommon and only turn up on the rare occasion. Do not be turned away from the breed, but be aware that if the breeder of your puppy is reputable and aware of these problems, he will be doing his utmost to keep them out of his line. Discuss all of these inherited problems with your chosen breeder before committing to the purchase of a puppy.

Due to the breed's long back, the Skye is predisposed to vertebral disk problems. Owners should limit the amount of step climbing that their dogs do. It's better to avoid steps entirely, but carpeting on steps makes them more manageable.

BREED STANDARD FOR THE
SKYE TERRIER

A prick-eared Skye of correct type, structure and balance.

As breeders started exhibiting at dog shows, it was realized that there must be more uniformity within each breed, i.e., all puppies in a litter should look alike as well as being of the same type as their sire and dam. Each breed approved by the American Kennel Club has a standard that gives the reader a mental picture of what the specific breed should look like. All reputable breeders strive to produce animals that will meet the requirements of the standard.

Many breeds were developed for a specific purpose, e.g., hunting, retrieving, going to ground, coursing, guarding, herding, etc. The Skye Terrier was bred to go to ground and to pursue vermin. In addition to having dogs that look like proper Skye Terriers, the standard assures that a Skye will act like a Skye Terrier, with the correct personality, disposition and character that are sought after in the breed.

Standards were originally written by fanciers who had a love and a concern for the breed. They knew that the essential characteristics of the Skye Terrier were unlike those of any other breed and that care must be taken so that these characteristics would be maintained through the generations.

THE AMERICAN KENNEL CLUB BREED STANDARD FOR THE SKYE TERRIER

General Appearance: The Skye Terrier is a dog of style, elegance and dignity: agile and strong with sturdy bone and hard muscle. Long, low and level—he is twice as long as he is high—he is covered with a profuse coat that falls straight down either side of the body over oval-shaped ribs. The hair well feathered on the head veils forehead and eyes to serve as protection from brush and briar as well as amid serious encounters with other animals. He stands with head high and long tail hanging and moves with a seemingly effortless gait. He is strong in body, quarter and jaw.

Size, Proportion, Substance: *Size*—The ideal shoulder height for dogs is 10 inches and bitches 9 1/2 inches. Based on these heights a 10-inch dog measured from chest bone over tail at rump should be 20 inches. A slightly higher or lower dog of either sex is acceptable. Dogs 9 inches or less and bitches 8 1/2 inches or less at the withers are to be penalized. *Proportion*—The ideal ratio of body length to shoulder height is 2 to 1, which is considered the correct proportion. *Substance*—Solidly built, full of strength and quality without being coarse. Bone is substantial.

Head: Long and powerful, strength being deemed more important than extreme length. *Eyes* brown, preferably dark brown, medium in size, close-set and alight with life and intelligence. *Ears* symmetrical and gracefully feathered. They may be carried prick or drop. If prick, they are medium in size, placed high on the skull, erect at their outer edges and slightly wider apart at the peak than at the skull. Drop ears, somewhat larger in size and set lower, hang flat against the skull.

Moderate width at the back of the skull tapers gradually to a strong muzzle. The stop is slight. The dark muzzle is just moderately full as opposed to snipy. Powerful and absolutely true jaws. The nose is always black. A Dudley, flesh-colored or brown nose shall disqualify. Mouth with the incisor teeth closing level, or with upper teeth slightly overlapping the lower.

Neck, Topline, Body: *Neck*—Long and gracefully arched, carried high and proudly. The backline is level. *Body* preeminently long and low, the chest deep, with oval-shaped ribs. The sides appear flattish due to the straight falling and profuse coat. *Tail* long and well feathered. When hanging, its upper section is pendulous, following the line of the rump, its lower section thrown back in a moderate arc without twist or curl. When raised, its height makes it appear a prolongation of the backline. Though not to be preferred, the tail is sometimes carried high when the dog is excited or angry. When such carriage arises from emotion only, it is permissible. But the tail should not be constantly carried above the level of the back or hang limp.

Forequarters: Shoulders well laid back, with tight placement of shoulder blades at the withers and elbows should fit closely to the sides and be neither loose nor tied. Forearm should curve slightly around the chest. Legs short, muscular and straight as possible.

SKYE TERRIER

The ears of Skye Terriers vary. On the left are correct drop ears. In the center are faulty ears, too far apart and carried off to the side. On the right are correct prick ears.

"Straight as possible" means straight as soundness and chest will permit, it does not mean "Terrier straight." *Feet*—Large hare-feet preferably pointing forward, the pads thick and nails strong and preferably black.

Hindquarters: Strong, full, well developed and well angulated. Legs short, muscular and straight when viewed from behind. Feet as in front.

This head study shows a prick-eared Skye of correct structure and type.

Coat: Double. Undercoat short, close, soft and woolly. Outer coat hard, straight and flat. Five and a half inches long without extra credit granted for greater length. The body coat hangs straight down each side, parting from head to tail. The head hair, which may be shorter, veils forehead and eyes and forms a moderate beard and apron. The long feathering on the ears falls straight down from the tips and outer edges, surrounding the ears like a fringe and outlining their shape. The ends of the hair should mingle with the coat of the neck. Tail well feathered.

Color: The coat must be of one overall color at the skin but may be of varying shades of the same color in the full coat, which may be black, blue, dark or light gray, silver platinum, fawn or cream. The dog must have no distinctive markings except for the desirable black points of ears, muzzle and tip of tail, all of which points are preferably dark even to black. The shade of head and legs should approximate that of the body. There must be no trace of pattern, design or clear-cut color variations, with the exception of the breed's only permissible white which occasionally exists on the chest not exceeding 2 inches in diameter.

The puppy coat may be very different in color from the adult coat. Therefore, as it is growing and clearing, wide variations of color may occur; consequently, this is permissible in dogs under 18 months of age. However, even in puppies there must be no trace of pattern, design or clear-cut variations with the exception of the black band encircling the body coat of the creme colored dog, and the only permissible white which, as in the adult dog, occasionally exists on the chest not exceeding 2 inches in diameter.

Gait: The legs proceed straight forward when traveling. When approaching, the forelegs form a continuation of the straight line of the front. The feet being the same distance apart as the elbows. The principal propelling power is furnished by the back legs which travel straight forward. Forelegs should move well forward, without too much lift. The whole movement may be termed free, active and effortless and give a more or less fluid picture.

Temperament: That of the typical working terrier capable of

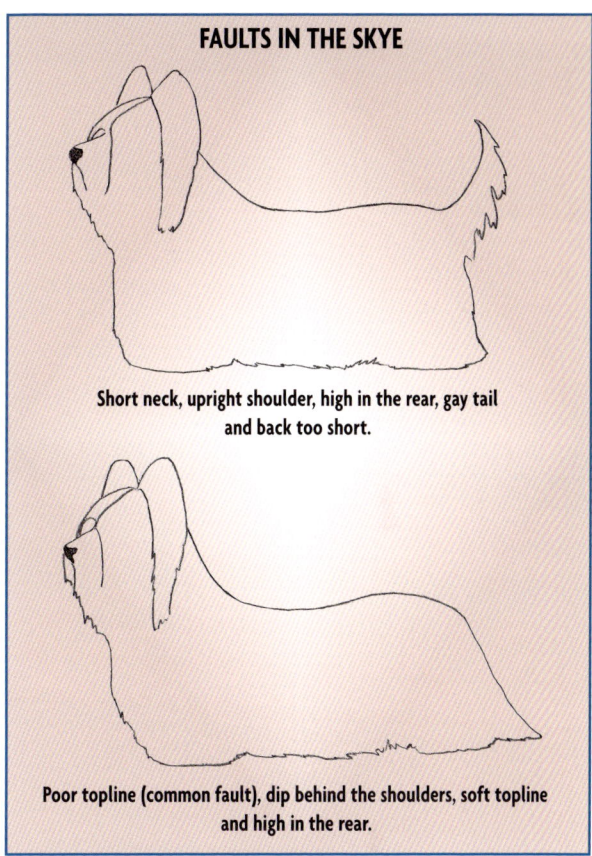

FAULTS IN THE SKYE

Short neck, upright shoulder, high in the rear, gay tail and back too short.

Poor topline (common fault), dip behind the shoulders, soft topline and high in the rear.

overtaking game and going to ground, displaying stamina, courage, strength and agility. Fearless, good-tempered, loyal and canny, he is friendly and gay with those he knows and reserved and cautious with strangers.

Disqualification: *A Dudley, flesh-colored or brown nose shall disqualify.*

Approved February 10, 1990
Effective March 28, 1990

YOUR PUPPY
SKYE TERRIER

WHERE TO BEGIN?

If you are convinced that the Skye Terrier is the ideal dog for you, it's time to learn about where to find a puppy and what to look for. Locating a litter of Skye Terrier tykes should not present a problem for the new owner, even though the breed is not as numerically strong as some of the other more popular terrier breeds. Terrier folk stick together and you can ask any terrier breeder whether he has friends who breed Skyes.

You should inquire about breeders who enjoy a good reputation in the breed. You are looking for an established breeder with outstanding dog ethics and a strong commitment to the breed. New owners should have as many questions as they have doubts. An established breeder is indeed the one to answer your four million questions and make you comfortable with your choice of the Skye. An established breeder will sell you a puppy at a fair price if, and only if, the breeder determines that you are a suitable, worthy owner of his dogs. An established breeder can be relied upon for advice, no matter what time of day or night, and will be knowledgeable and forthright when it comes to discussing the health problems that concern the breed. A reputable breeder will accept a puppy back, without questions, should you decide that this is not the right dog for you.

Choosing a breeder is an important first step in dog owner-

> **SIGNS OF A HEALTHY PUPPY**
> Healthy puppies are robust little fellows who are alert and active, sporting shiny coats and supple skin. They should not appear lethargic, bloated or pot-bellied, nor should they have flaky skin or runny or crusted eyes or noses. Their stools should be firm and well formed, with no evidence of blood or mucus.

ship. Fortunately, Skye breeders are a tightly knit, professional group of dog fanciers who are astutely devoted to the breed and its well-being. New owners should have little problem finding a reputable breeder who doesn't live on the other side of the country. The American Kennel Club is able to recommend breeders of quality Skye Terriers, as can the national Skye club or any local all-breed club.

Potential owners are encouraged to attend dog shows (or trials) to see the Skyes in action, to meet the owners and handlers firsthand and to get an idea of what Skye Terriers look like outside a photographer's lens. Provided you approach the handlers when they are not terribly busy with the dogs, most are more than willing to answer questions, recommend breeders and give advice.

Once you have contacted and met a breeder or two and made your choice about which breeder is best suited to your needs, it's time to visit the litter. Keep in mind that the top breeders will have waiting lists. Depending on what kind of puppy is required, sometimes new owners have to wait as long as two years for a puppy. If you are really committed to the breeder whom you've selected and the sex, color, ear style, etc., that you want in a pup, then you will wait (and hope for an early arrival!). If you are willing to compromise, then your puppy may come a bit faster. However, *never* compromise when it comes to the quality of the pup and the reputation of the breeder.

Since you are likely to be choosing a Skye as a pet dog and not a show dog, you simply

MAKE A COMMITMENT
Dogs are most assuredly man's best friend, but they are also a lot of work. When you add a puppy to your family, you also are adding to your daily responsibilities for years to come. Dogs need more than just food, water and a place to sleep. They also require training (which can be ongoing throughout the lifetime of the dog), activity to keep them physically and mentally fit and hands-on attention every day, plus grooming and healthcare. Your life as you now know it may well disappear! Are you prepared for such drastic changes?

Most likely the breeder will not allow you to see the litter when the pups are this young. Still sleeping in piles, these three-week-olds are snuggling close for warmth.

around the eighth week. Breeders spend significant amounts of time with the Skye toddlers so that the pups are able to interact with the "other species," i.e., humans. Given the long history that dogs and humans have, bonding between the two species is natural but must be nurtured.

should select a pup that is friendly, attractive and sound. Always check the bite of your selected puppy to be sure that it is neither overshot nor undershot. This may not be too noticeable on a young puppy but will become more evident as the puppy gets older. Sometimes a slightly off bite corrects itself; sometimes it worsens.

Breeders commonly allow visitors to see their litters by around the fifth or sixth week, and puppies leave for their new homes between the eighth and tenth week. Puppies need to learn the rules of the pack from their dams, and most dams continue teaching the pups manners and dos and don'ts until

PEDIGREE VS. REGISTRATION CERTIFICATE

Too often new owners are confused between these two important documents. Your puppy's pedigree, essentially a family tree, is a written record of a dog's genealogy of three generations or more. The pedigree will show you the names as well as performance titles of all dogs in your pup's background. Your breeder must provide you with a registration application, with his part properly filled out. You must complete the application and send it to the AKC with the proper fee. Every puppy must come from a litter that has been AKC-registered by the breeder, born in the US and from a sire and dam that are also registered with the AKC.

The seller must provide you with complete records to identify the puppy. The AKC requires that the seller provide the buyer with the following: breed; sex, color and markings; date of birth; litter number (when available); names and registration numbers of the parents; breeder's name; and date sold or delivered.

Puppy

A well-bred, well-socialized Skye pup wants nothing more than to be near you.

A COMMITTED NEW OWNER

By now you should understand what makes the Skye Terrier a most unique and special dog, one that may fit nicely into your family and lifestyle. If you have researched breeders, you should be able to recognize a knowledgeable and responsible Skye Terrier breeder who cares not only about his pups but also about what kind of owner you will be. If you have completed the final step in your new journey, you have found a litter, or possibly two, of quality Skye Terrier pups.

A visit with the puppies and their breeder should be an education in itself. Breed research, breeder selection and puppy visitation are very important aspects of finding the puppy of your dreams. Beyond that, these things also lay the foundation for a successful future with your pup. Puppy personalities within each litter vary, from the shy and easy-going puppy to the one who is dominant and assertive, with most pups falling somewhere in between. By spending time with the puppies you will be able to recognize certain behaviors and what these behaviors indicate about each pup's temperament. Which type of pup will complement your family dynamics is best determined by observing the puppies in action within their "pack." Your breeder's expertise and recommendations are also valuable. Although you may fall in love with a bold and brassy

NEW RELEASES
Most breeders release their puppies between eight to ten weeks of age. A breeder who allows puppies to leave the litter at five or six weeks of age may be more concerned with profit than with the puppies' welfare. However, some breeders of show or working breeds may hold one or more top-quality puppies longer, occasionally until three or four months of age, in order to evaluate the puppies' career or show potential and decide which one(s) they will keep for themselves.

Puppies inherit many traits, both in looks and temperament, from their parents. Observing at least one of the parents is an aid in predicting how the puppies of a litter will mature.

male, the breeder may suggest that another pup would be best for you. The breeder's experience in rearing Skye Terrier pups and matching their temperaments with appropriate humans offers the best assurance that your pup will meet your needs and expectations. The type of puppy that you select is just as important as your decision that the Skye Terrier is the breed for you.

The decision to live with a Skye Terrier is a serious commitment and not one to be taken lightly. This puppy is a living sentient being that will be dependent on you for basic survival for his entire life. Beyond the basics of survival—food, water, shelter and protection—he needs much, much more. The new pup needs love, nurturing and a proper canine education to mold him into a responsible, well-behaved canine citizen. Your Skye Terrier's health and good manners will need consistent monitoring and regular "tune-ups," so your job as a responsible dog owner will be ongoing throughout every stage of his life. If you are not prepared to accept these responsibilities and commit to them for the next decade, likely longer, then you are not prepared to own a dog of any breed.

Although the responsibilities of owning a dog may at times tax your patience, the joy of living with your Skye Terrier far outweighs the workload, and a well-mannered adult dog is worth your time and effort. Before your

FINDING A QUALIFIED BREEDER

Before you begin your puppy search, ask your veterinarian and perhaps other breeders to refer you to someone they believe is reputable. Responsible breeders usually raise only one or two breeds of dog. Avoid any breeder who has several different breeds or has several litters at the same time. Dedicated breeders are usually involved with a breed or other dog club. Many participate in some sport or activity related to their breed. Just as you want to be assured of the breeder's qualifications, the breeder wants to be assured that you will make a worthy owner. Expect the breeder to interview you, asking questions about your goals for the pup, your experience with dogs and what kind of home you will provide.

Puppy

It's not easy to select a puppy from a litter of healthy, happy and well-bred Skye puppies, as one is as cute and irresistible as the next!

very eyes, your new charge will grow up to be your most loyal friend, devoted to you unconditionally.

YOUR SKYE TERRIER SHOPPING LIST

Just as expectant parents prepare a nursery for their baby, so should you ready your home for the arrival of your Skye Terrier pup. If you have the necessary puppy supplies purchased and in place before he comes home, it will ease the puppy's transition from the warmth and familiarity of his mom and littermates to the brand-new environment of his new home and human family. You will be too busy to stock up and prepare your house after your pup comes home, that's for sure! Imagine how a pup must feel upon being transported to a strange new place. It's up to you to comfort him and to let your little pup know that he is going to be happy with you.

FOOD AND WATER BOWLS

Your puppy will need separate bowls for his food and water. Stainless steel pans are generally preferred over plastic bowls since they sterilize better and pups are less inclined to chew

---

MALE OR FEMALE?

Males of most dog breeds tend to be larger than their female counterparts and take longer to mature. Males also can be more dominant and territorial, especially if they are intact. Neutering before one year of age can help minimize those tendencies. Females of most breeds are often less rambunctious and easier to handle. However, individual personalities vary, so the differences are often due more to temperament than to the sex of the animal.

SKYE TERRIER

The three most popular crate types: mesh on the left, wire on the right and fiberglass on top.

ments, the benefits of crate use are many. The crate provides the puppy with his very own "safe house," a cozy place to sleep, take a break or seek comfort with a favorite toy; a travel aid to house your dog when on the road, at motels or at the vet's office; a training aid to help teach your puppy proper toileting habits; and a place of solitude when non-dog people happen to drop by and don't want a lively puppy—or even a well-behaved adult dog—saying hello or begging for attention.

Crates come in several types, although the wire crate and the fiberglass airline-type crate are the most popular. Both are safe and your puppy will adjust to either one, so the choice is up to you. The wire crates offer better visibility for the pup as well as better ventilation. Many of the wire crates easily fold into suitcase-size carriers. The fiberglass crates, similar to those used by the airlines for animal transport, are sturdier and more den-like. However, the fiberglass crates do not fold down and are less ventilated than a wire crate, which can be problematic in hot weather. Some of the newer crates are made of heavy plastic mesh; they are very lightweight and fold up into slim-line suitcases. However, a mesh crate might not be suitable for a pup with manic chewing habits.

on the metal. Heavy-duty ceramic bowls are popular, but consider how often you will have to pick up those heavy bowls. Buy adult-sized pans, as your puppy will grow into them before you know it.

THE DOG CRATE

If you think that crates are tools of punishment and confinement for when a dog has misbehaved, think again. Most breeders and almost all trainers recommend a crate as the preferred house-training aid as well as for all-around puppy training and safety. Because dogs are natural den creatures that prefer cave-like environ-

Don't bother with a puppy-sized crate. Although your Skye Terrier will be a little fellow when you bring him home, he will grow up in the blink of an eye and your puppy crate will be useless. Purchase a crate that will accommodate an adult Skye Terrier. Although the Skye is not a tall dog, it is a long dog, and a large crate will be necessary for a fully-grown Skye to stretch and be comfortable inside his crate.

BEDDING AND CRATE PADS
Your puppy will enjoy some type of soft bedding in his "room" (the crate), something he can snuggle into to feel cozy and secure. Old towels or blankets are good choices for a young pup, since he may (and probably will) have a toileting accident or two in the crate or decide to chew on the bedding material. Once he is fully trained and out of the early chewing stage, you can replace the puppy bedding with a permanent crate pad if you prefer. Crate pads and other dog beds run the gamut from inexpensive to high-end doggie-designer styles, but don't splurge on the good stuff until you are sure that your puppy is reliable and won't tear it up or make a mess on it.

> **CRATE EXPECTATIONS**
> To make the crate more inviting to your puppy, you can offer his first meal or two inside the crate, always keeping the crate door open so that he does not feel confined. Keep a favorite toy or two in the crate for him to play with while inside. You can also cover the crate at night with a lightweight sheet to make it more den-like and remove the stimuli of household activity. Never put him into his crate as punishment or as you are scolding him, since he will then associate his crate with negative situations and avoid going there.

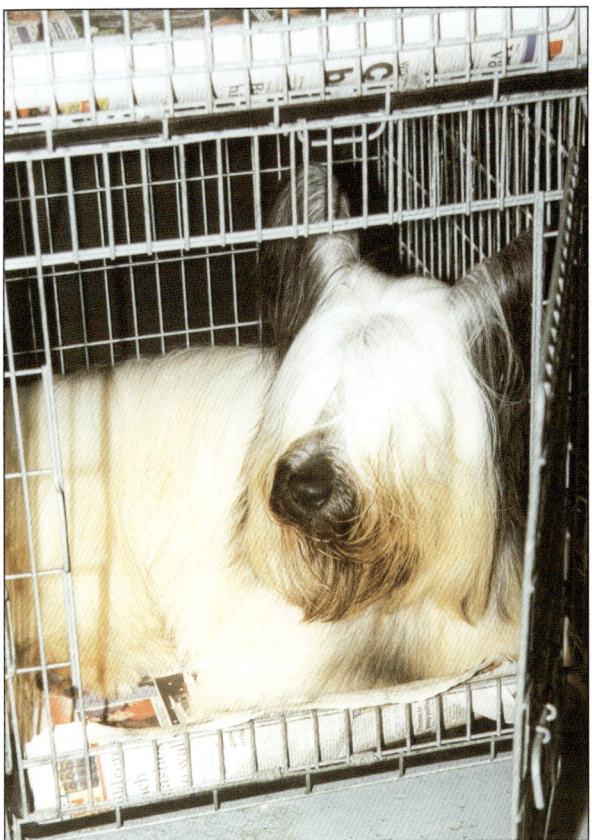

Once the Skye is fully-grown, he will regard his crate as his own den, where he feels safe and "on his own."

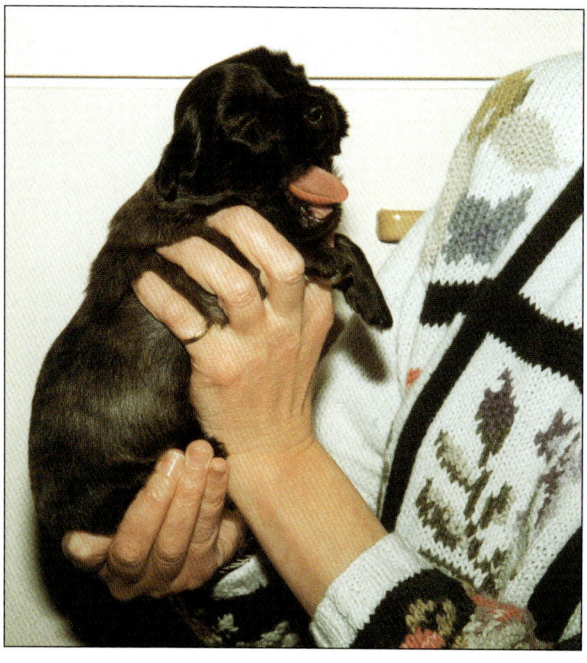

At only a couple of weeks old, this Skye is a tiny pup in a big world. He still has about two more months with the breeder and his littermates before he will be ready to go to his new home.

PUPPY TOYS

Just as infants and older children require objects to stimulate their minds and bodies, puppies need toys to entertain their curious brains, wiggly paws and achy teeth. A fun array of safe doggie toys will help satisfy your puppy's chewing instincts and distract him from gnawing on the leg of your antique chair or your new leather sofa. Most puppy toys are cute and look as if they would be a lot of fun, but not all are necessarily safe or good for your puppy, so use caution when you go puppy-toy shopping.

Skye puppies are fairly aggressive chewers and only the hardest, strongest toys should be offered to them. The best "chewcifiers" are nylon and hard rubber bones, which are safe to gnaw on and come in sizes appropriate for all age groups and breeds. Be especially careful of natural bones, which can splinter or develop dangerous sharp edges; pups can easily swallow or choke on those bone splinters. Veterinarians often tell of surgical nightmares involving bits of splintered bone, because in addition to the danger of choking, the sharp pieces can damage the intestinal tract.

Similarly, rawhide chews, while a favorite of most dogs and puppies, can be equally dangerous. Pieces of rawhide are easily swallowed after they get soft and

> **SOME DAM ATTITUDE**
> When selecting a puppy, be certain to meet the dam of the litter. The temperament of the dam is often predictive of the temperament of her puppies. However, dams occasionally are very protective of their young, some to the point of being testy or aggressive with visitors, whom they may view as a danger to their babies. Such attitudes are more common when the pups are very young and still nursing and should not be mistaken for an actual aggressive temperament. If possible, visit the dam away from her pups to make friends with her and gain a better understanding of her true personality.

gummy from chewing, and dogs have been known to choke on pieces of ingested rawhide. Rawhide chews should be offered only when you can supervise the puppy.

Soft woolly toys are special puppy favorites. They come in a wide variety of cute shapes and sizes; some look like little stuffed animals. Puppies love to shake them up and toss them about or simply carry them around. Be careful of fuzzy toys that have button eyes or noses that your pup could chew off and swallow, and make sure that he does not disembowel a squeaky toy to remove the squeaker! Braided rope toys are similar in that they are fun to chew and toss around, but they shred easily and the strings are easy to swallow. The strings are not digestible and, if the puppy doesn't pass them in his stool, he could end up at the vet's office. As with rawhides, your puppy should be closely monitored with rope toys.

If you believe that your pup has ingested a piece of one of his toys, check his stools for the next couple of days to see if he passes the item when he defecates. At the same time, also watch for signs of intestinal distress. A call to your veterinarian might be in order to get his advice and be on the safe side.

An all-time favorite toy for puppies (young and old!) is the

TOYS 'R SAFE

The vast array of tantalizing puppy toys is staggering. Stroll through any pet shop or pet-supply outlet and you will see that the choices can be overwhelming. However, not all dog toys are safe or sensible. Most very young puppies enjoy soft woolly toys that they can snuggle with and carry around. (You know they have outgrown them when they shred them up!) Avoid toys that have buttons, tabs or other enhancements that can be chewed off and swallowed. Soft toys that squeak are fun, but make sure your puppy does not disembowel the toy and remove (and swallow) the squeaker. Toys that rattle or make noise can excite a puppy, but they present the same danger as the squeaky kind and so require supervision. Hard rubber toys that bounce can also entertain a pup, but make sure that the toy is too big for your pup to swallow.

The Skye puppy you select should be alert and responsive. Who could resist the bunny-appeal of this sprightly urchin?

empty gallon milk jug. Hard plastic juice containers—46 ounces or more—are also excellent. Such containers make lots of noise when they are batted about, and puppies go crazy with delight as they play with them. However, they don't often last very long, so be sure to remove and replace them when they get chewed up.

A word of caution about homemade toys: be careful with your choices of non-traditional play objects. Never use old shoes or socks, since a puppy cannot distinguish between the old ones on which he's allowed to chew and the new ones in your closet that are strictly off limits. That principle applies to anything that resembles something that you don't want your puppy to chew.

COLLARS

A lightweight nylon collar is the best choice for a very young pup. Quick-click collars are easy to put on and remove, and they can be adjusted as the puppy grows. Introduce him to his collar as soon as he comes home to get him accustomed to wearing it. He'll get used to it quickly and won't mind a bit. Make sure that it is snug enough that it won't slip off yet loose enough to be comfortable for the pup. You should be able to slip two fingers between the collar and his neck. Check the collar often, as puppies grow in spurts, and his collar can become too tight almost overnight. Choke collars are made for training but are not recommended for use on small dogs and coated breeds. A choke collar will pull and damage the Skye's long coat.

LEASHES

A 6-foot nylon lead is an excellent choice for a young puppy. It is lightweight and not as tempting to chew as a leather lead. You can switch to a 6-foot leather lead after your pup has grown and is used to walking politely on a lead. For initial puppy walks and house-training purposes, you should invest in a shorter lead so that you have more control over the puppy. At first, you don't want him wandering too far away from you, and when taking him out for toileting you will want to keep him in the specific area chosen for his potty spot.

Once the puppy is heel-trained with a traditional leash, you can consider purchasing a retractable lead. A retractable lead is excellent for walking adult dogs that are already leash-wise. This type of lead allows the dog to roam farther away from you and explore a wider area when out walking, and also retracts when you need to keep him close to you.

HOME SAFETY FOR YOUR PUPPY

The importance of puppy-proofing cannot be overstated. In addition to making your house comfortable for your Skye Terrier's arrival, you also must make sure that your house is safe for your puppy before you bring him home. There are countless hazards in the owner's personal living environment that a pup can sniff, chew, swallow or destroy. Many are obvious; others are not. Do a thorough advance house check to remove or rearrange those things that could hurt your puppy, keeping any potentially dangerous items out of areas to which he will have access.

Electrical cords are especially dangerous, since puppies view them as irresistible chew toys. Unplug and remove all exposed cords or fasten them beneath base-

TEETHING TIME
All puppies chew. It's normal canine behavior. Chewing just plain feels good to a puppy, especially during the three- to five-month teething period when the adult teeth are breaking through the gums. Rather than attempting to eliminate such a strong natural chewing instinct, you will be more successful if you redirect it and teach your puppy what he may or may not chew. Correct inappropriate chewing with a sharp "No!" and offer him a chew toy, praising him when he takes it. Don't become discouraged. Chewing usually decreases after the adult teeth have come in.

boards where the puppy cannot reach them. Veterinarians and firefighters can tell you horror stories about electrical burns and house fires that resulted from puppy-chewed electrical cords. Consider this a most serious precaution for your puppy and the rest of your family.

Scout your home for tiny objects that might be seen at a pup's eye level. Keep medication bottles and cleaning supplies well out of reach, and do the same with waste baskets and other trash containers. It goes without saying that you should not use rodent poison or other toxic chemicals in any puppy area and that you must keep such containers safely locked up. You will be amazed at how many places a curious puppy can discover!

Once your house has cleared inspection, check your yard. A sturdy fence, well embedded into the ground, will give your dog a safe place to play and potty.

Although Skye Terriers are not known to be climbers or fence jumpers, they are still athletic dogs, so a 5- to 6-foot-high fence should be adequate to contain an agile youngster or adult. Check the fence periodically for necessary repairs. If there is a weak link or space to squeeze through, you can be sure a determined Skye Terrier will discover it.

The garage and shed can be hazardous places for a pup, as things like fertilizers, chemicals and tools are usually kept there. It's best to keep these areas off limits to the pup. Antifreeze is especially dangerous to dogs, as they find the taste appealing, and it takes only a few licks from the driveway to kill a dog, puppy or adult, small breed or large.

VISITING THE VETERINARIAN

A good veterinarian is your Skye Terrier puppy's best health-insurance policy. If you do not already have a vet, ask friends and experienced dog people in your area for recommendations so that you can select a vet before you bring your Skye Terrier puppy home. Also arrange for your puppy's first veterinary examination beforehand, since many vets do not have appointments immediately available, and your puppy should visit the vet within a day or so of coming home.

It's important to make sure your puppy's first visit to the vet

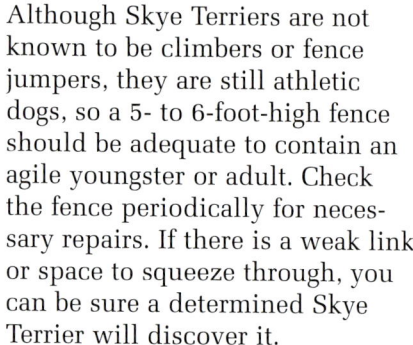

COST OF OWNERSHIP
The purchase price of your puppy is merely the first expense in the typical dog budget. Quality dog food, veterinary care (sickness and health maintenance), dog supplies and grooming costs will add up to big bucks every year. Can you adequately afford to support a canine addition to the family?

A Dog-Safe Home

The dog-safety police are taking you on a house tour. Let's go room by room and see how safe your own home is for your new Skye Terrier. The following items are doggy dangers, so either they must be removed or the dog should be monitored or not have access to these areas.

Living Room
- house plants (some varieties are poisonous)
- fireplace or wood-burning stove
- paint on the walls (lead-based paint is toxic)
- lead drapery weights (toxic lead)
- lamps and electrical cords
- carpet cleaners or deodorizers

Outdoor
- swimming pool
- pesticides
- toxic plants
- lawn fertilizers

Bathroom
- blue water in the toilet bowl
- medicine cabinet (filled with potentially deadly bottles)
- soap bars, bleach, drain cleaners, etc.
- tampons

Kitchen
- household cleaners in the kitchen cabinets
- glass jars and canisters
- sharp objects (like kitchen knives, scissors and forks)
- garbage can (with remnants of good-smelling things like onions, potato skins, apple or pear cores, peach pits, coffee beans, etc.)
- "people foods" that are toxic to dogs, like chocolate, raisins, grapes, nuts and onions

Garage
- antifreeze
- fertilizers (including rose foods)
- pesticides and rodenticides
- pool supplies (chlorine and other chemicals)
- oil and gasoline in containers
- sharp objects, electrical cords and power tools

Skye puppies are curious little tykes and will sample anything they find. Be careful where you leave dangerous (and important) items.

is a pleasant and positive one. The vet should take great care to befriend the pup and handle him gently to make their first meeting a positive experience. The vet will give the pup a thorough physical examination and set up a schedule for vaccinations and other necessary wellness visits. Be sure to show your vet any health and inoculation records, which you should have received from your breeder. Your vet is a great source of canine health information, so be sure to ask questions and take notes. Creating a health journal for your puppy will make a handy reference for his wellness and any future health problems that may arise.

MEETING THE FAMILY

Your Skye Terrier's homecoming is an exciting time for all members of the family, and it's only natural that everyone will be eager to meet him, pet him and play with him. However, for the puppy's sake, it's best to make these initial family meetings as uneventful as possible so that the pup is not overwhelmed with too much too soon. Remember, he has just left his dam and his littermates and is away from the breeder's home for the first time. Despite his fuzzy wagging tail, he is still apprehensive and wondering where he is and who all these strange humans are. It's best to let him explore on his own and meet the family members as he feels comfortable. Let him investigate all the new smells, sights and sounds at his own pace. Children should be especially careful to not get overly excited, use loud voices or hug the pup too tightly. Be calm, gentle and affectionate, and be

KEEP OUT OF REACH

Most dogs don't browse around your medicine cabinet, but accidents do happen! The drug acetaminophen, the active ingredient in certain popular over-the-counter pain relievers, can be deadly to dogs and cats if ingested in large quantities. Acetaminophen toxicity, caused by the dog's swallowing 15 to 20 tablets, can be manifested in abdominal pains within a day or two of ingestion, as well as liver damage. If you suspect your dog has swiped a bottle of medication, get the dog to the vet immediately so that the vet can induce vomiting and cleanse the dog's stomach.

ready to comfort him if he appears frightened or uneasy.

Be sure to show your puppy his new crate during this first day home. Toss a treat or two inside the crate; if he associates the crate with food, he will associate the crate with good things. If he is comfortable with the crate, you can offer him his first meal inside it. Leave the door ajar so he can wander in and out as he chooses.

FIRST NIGHT IN HIS NEW HOME
So much has happened in your Skye Terrier puppy's first day away from the breeder. He's likely had his first car ride to his new home. He's met his new human family and perhaps the other family pets. He has explored his new house and yard, at least those places where he is to be allowed during his first weeks at home. He may have visited his new veterinarian. He has eaten his first meal or two away from his dam and littermates. Surely that's enough to tire out an eight-week-old Skye Terrier pup—or so you hope!

It's bedtime. During the day, the pup investigated his crate, which is his new den and sleeping space, so it is not entirely strange to him. Line the crate with a soft towel or blanket that he can snuggle into and gently place him into the crate for the night. Some breeders send home a piece of bedding from where the pup slept

TOXIC PLANTS
Plants are natural puppy magnets, but many can be harmful, even fatal, if ingested by a puppy or adult dog. Scout your yard and home interior and remove any plants, bushes or flowers that could be even mildly dangerous. It could save your puppy's life. You can obtain a complete list of toxic plants from your veterinarian, at the public library or by looking online.

with his littermates, and those familiar scents are a great comfort for the puppy on his first night without his siblings.

He will probably whine or cry. The puppy is objecting to the confinement and the fact that he is alone for the first time. This can be a stressful time for you as well as for the pup. It's important that you remain strong and don't let the puppy out of his crate to comfort him. He will fall asleep eventually. If you release him, the puppy will learn that crying means "out" and will continue

Even when relaxing, this Skye puppy is keen, alert and ready to go.

that habit. You are laying the groundwork for future habits. Some breeders find that soft music can soothe a crying pup and help him get to sleep.

SOCIALIZING YOUR PUPPY
The first 20 weeks of your Skye Terrier puppy's life are the most important of his entire lifetime. A properly socialized puppy will grow up to be a confident and stable adult who will be a pleasure to live with and a welcome addition to the neighborhood.

The importance of socialization cannot be overemphasized. Research on canine behavior has proven that puppies who are not exposed to new sights, sounds, people and animals during their first 20 weeks of life will grow up to be timid and fearful, even aggressive, and unable to flourish outside of their familiar home environment.

Socializing your puppy is not difficult and, in fact, will be a fun time for you both. Lead training goes hand in hand with socialization, so your puppy will be learning how to walk on a lead at the same time that he's meeting the neighborhood. Because the Skye Terrier is such a unique, irresistible breed, everyone will enjoy meeting "the new kid on the block." Take him for short walks, to the park and to other dog-friendly places where he will encounter new people, especially children. Puppies automatically

---

FIRST CAR RIDE
The ride to your home from the breeder will no doubt be your puppy's first automobile experience, and you should make every effort to keep him comfortable and secure. Bring a large towel or small blanket for the puppy to lie on during the trip and an extra towel in case the pup gets carsick or has a potty accident. It's best to have another person with you to hold the puppy in his lap. Most puppies will fall fast asleep from the rolling motion of the car. If the ride is lengthy, you may have to stop so that the puppy can relieve himself, so be sure to bring a leash and collar for those stops. Avoid rest areas for potty trips, since those are frequented by many dogs, who may carry parasites or disease. It's better to stop at grassy areas near gas stations or shopping centers to prevent unhealthy exposure for your pup.

recognize children as "little people" and are drawn to play with them. Just make sure that you supervise these meetings and that the children do not get too rough or encourage him to play too hard. An overzealous pup can often nip too hard, frightening the child and in turn making the puppy overly excited. A bad experience in puppyhood can impact a dog for life, so a pup that has a negative experience with a child may grow up to be shy or even aggressive around children.

Take your puppy along on your daily errands. Puppies are natural "people magnets," and most people who see your pup will want to pet him. All of these encounters will help to mold him into a confident adult dog. Likewise, you will soon feel like a confident, responsible dog owner, rightly proud of your mannerly Skye Terrier.

Be especially careful of your puppy's encounters and experiences during the eight-to-ten-week-old period, which is also called the "fear period." This is a serious imprinting period, and all contact during this time should be gentle and positive. A frightening or negative event could leave a permanent impression that could affect his future behavior if a similar situation arises.

Also make sure that your puppy has received his first and second rounds of vaccinations before you expose him to other dogs or bring him to places that other dogs may frequent. Avoid dog parks and other strange-dog areas until your vet assures you that your puppy is fully immunized and resistant to the diseases that can be passed between canines. Discuss socialization with your breeder, as some breeders recommend socializing the puppy even before he has received all of his inoculations, depending on how outgoing the breed or puppy may be.

LEADER OF THE PUPPY'S PACK

Like other canines, your puppy needs an authority figure, someone he can look up to and regard as the leader of his "pack." His first pack leader was his dam, who taught him to be polite and not chew too hard on her ears or

You can learn quite a bit about the puppies' future temperaments by observing them at play with their littermates.

nip at her muzzle. He learned those same lessons from his littermates. If he played too rough, they cried in pain and stopped the game, which sent an important message to the rowdy puppy.

As puppies play together, they are also struggling to determine who will be the boss. Being pack animals, dogs need someone to be in charge. If a litter of puppies remained together beyond puppyhood, one of the pups would emerge as the strongest one, the one who calls the shots.

Once your puppy leaves the pack, he will look intuitively for a new leader. If he does not recognize you as that leader, he will try to assume that position for himself. Of course, it is hard to imagine your adorable Skye Terrier puppy trying to be in charge when he is so small and seemingly helpless. You must remember that these are natural canine instincts. Do not cave in and allow your pup to get the upper "paw"!

Just as socialization is so important during these first 20 weeks, so too is your puppy's early education. He was born without any bad habits. He does not know what is good or bad behavior. If he does things like nipping and digging, it's because he is having fun and doesn't know that humans consider these things as "bad." It's your job to teach him proper puppy manners, and this is the best time to accomplish that—before he has developed bad habits, since it is much more difficult to "unlearn" or correct unacceptable learned behavior than to teach good behavior from the start.

Make sure that all members of the family understand the importance of being consistent when training their new puppy. If you tell the puppy to stay off the sofa and your daughter allows him to cuddle on the couch to watch her favorite television show, your pup will be confused about what he is and is not allowed to do. Have a family conference before your pup comes home so that everyone understands the basic principles of puppy training and the rules

THE CRITICAL SOCIALIZATION PERIOD

Canine research has shown that a puppy's 8th through 16th week is the most critical learning period of his life. This is when the puppy "learns to learn," a time when he needs positive experiences to build confidence and stability. Puppies who are not exposed to different people and situations outside the home during this period can grow up to be fearful and sometimes aggressive. This is also the best time for puppy lessons, since he has not yet acquired any bad habits that could undermine his ability to learn.

> **BE CONSISTENT**
>
> Consistency is a key element, in fact is absolutely necessary, to a puppy's learning environment. A behavior (such as chewing, jumping up or climbing onto the furniture) cannot be forbidden one day and then allowed the next. That will only confuse the pup, and he will not understand what he is supposed to do. Just one or two episodes of allowing an undesirable behavior to "slide" will imprint that behavior on a puppy's brain and make that behavior more difficult to erase or change.

you have set forth for the pup and agrees to follow them.

The old saying that "an ounce of prevention is worth a pound of cure" is especially true when it comes to puppies. It is much easier to prevent inappropriate behavior than it is to change it. It's also easier and less stressful for the pup, since it will keep discipline to a minimum and create a more positive learning environment for him. That, in turn, will also be easier on you!

Here are a few commonsense tips to keep your belongings safe and your puppy out of trouble:
- Keep your closet doors closed and your shoes, socks and other apparel off the floor so your puppy can't get to them.
- Keep a secure lid on the trash container or put the trash where your puppy can't dig into it. He can't damage what he can't reach!
- Supervise your puppy at all times to make sure he is not getting into mischief. If he starts to chew the corner of the rug, you can distract him instantly by tossing a toy for him to fetch. You also will be able to whisk him outside when you notice that he is about to piddle on the carpet. If you can't see your puppy, you can't teach him or correct his behavior.

SOLVING PUPPY PROBLEMS

CHEWING AND NIPPING
Nipping at fingers and toes is normal puppy behavior. Chewing is also the way that puppies investigate their surroundings.

If your Skye has been properly socialized, he will accept pups and adult dogs alike into his company.

However, you will have to teach your puppy that chewing anything other than his toys is not acceptable. That won't happen overnight and at times puppy teeth will test your patience. However, if you allow nipping and chewing to continue, just think about the damage that a mature Skye Terrier can do with a full set of adult teeth.

Whenever your puppy nips your hand or fingers, cry out "Ouch!" in a loud voice, which should startle your puppy and stop him from nipping, even if only for a moment. Immediately distract him by offering a small treat or an appropriate toy for him to chew instead (which means having chew toys and puppy treats handy or in your pockets at all times). Praise him when he takes the toy and tell him what a good fellow he is. Praise is just as or even more important in puppy training as discipline and correction.

Puppies also tend to nip at children more often than adults, since they perceive little ones to be more vulnerable and more similar to their littermates. Teach your children appropriate responses to nipping behavior. If they are unable to handle it themselves, you may have to intervene. Puppy nips can be quite painful and a child's frightened reaction will only encourage a puppy to nip harder, which is a natural canine response. As with all other puppy situations, interaction between your Skye Terrier puppy and children should be supervised.

Chewing on objects, not just family members' fingers and ankles, is also normal canine behavior that can be especially tedious (for the owner, not the pup) during the teething period when the puppy's adult teeth are coming in. At this stage, chewing just plain feels good. Furniture legs and cabinet corners are common puppy favorites. Shoes and other personal items also taste pretty good to a pup.

The best solution is, once again, prevention. If you value something, keep it tucked away and out of reach. You can't hide your dining-room table in a closet, but you can try to deflect the chewing by applying a bitter product made just to deter dogs from chewing. Available in a spray or cream, this substance is vile-tasting, although safe for

ESTABLISH A ROUTINE

Routine is very important to a puppy's learning environment. To facilitate house-training, use the same exit/entrance door for potty trips and always take the puppy to the same place in the yard. The same principle of consistency applies to all other aspects of puppy training.

dogs, and most puppies will avoid the forbidden object after one tiny taste. You also can apply the product to your leather leash if the puppy tries to chew on his lead during leash-training sessions.

Keep a ready supply of safe chews handy to offer your Skye Terrier as a distraction when he starts to chew on something that's a "no-no." Remember, at this tender age, he does not yet know what is permitted or forbidden, so you have to be "on call" every minute he's awake and on the prowl.

You may lose a treasure or two during your puppy's growing-up period, and the furniture could sustain a nasty nick or two. These can be trying times, so be prepared for those inevitable accidents and comfort yourself in knowing that this too shall pass.

PUPPY WHINING
Puppies often cry and whine, just as infants and little children do. It's their way of telling us that they are lonely or in need of attention. Your puppy will miss his littermates and will feel insecure when he is left alone. You may be out of the house or just in another room, but he will still feel alone. During these times, the puppy's crate should be his personal comfort station, a place all his own where he can feel safe and secure. Once he learns that being alone is okay and not something to be feared, he will settle down without crying or objecting. You might want to leave a radio on while he is crated, as the sound of human voices can be soothing and will give the impression that people are around.

Give your puppy a favorite cuddly toy or chew toy to entertain him whenever he is crated. You will both be happier: the puppy because he is safe in his den and you because he is quiet, safe and not getting into puppy escapades that can wreak havoc in your house or cause him danger.

To make sure that your puppy will always view his crate as a safe and cozy place, never, ever use the crate as punishment. That's the best way to turn the crate into a negative place that the pup will want to avoid. Sure, you can use the crate for your own peace of mind if your puppy is getting into trouble and needs some "time out." Just don't let him know that. Never scold the pup and immediately place him into the crate. Count to ten, give him a couple of hugs and maybe a treat, then scoot him into his crate.

It's also important not to make a big fuss when he is released from the crate. That will make getting out of the crate more appealing than being in the crate, which is just the opposite of what you are trying to achieve.

PROPER CARE OF YOUR SKYE TERRIER

Adding a Skye Terrier to your household means adding a new family member who will need your care each and every day. When your Skye Terrier pup first comes home, you will start a routine with him so that, as he grows up, your dog will have a daily schedule just as you do. The aspects of your dog's daily care will likewise become regular parts of your day, so you'll both have a new schedule. Dogs learn by consistency and thrive on routine: regular times for meals, exercise, grooming and potty trips are just as important for your dog as they are for you! Your dog's schedule will depend much on your family's daily routine, but remember that you now have a new member of the family who is part of your day every day!

FEEDING

Feeding your dog the best diet is based on various factors, including age, activity level, overall condition and size of breed. When you visit the breeder, he will share with you his advice about the proper diet for your dog based on his experience with the breed and the foods with which he has had success. Likewise, your vet will be a helpful source of advice throughout the dog's life and will aid you in planning a diet for optimal health.

Feeding the Puppy

Of course, your pup's very first food will be his dam's milk. There may be special situations in which pups fail to nurse, necessitating that the breeder hand-feed them with a formula, but for the most part pups spend the first weeks of life nursing from their dam. The breeder weans the pups

> **JUST ADD MEAT**
> An organic alternative to the traditional dog kibble or canned food comes in the form of grain-based feeds. These dry cereal-type products consist of oat and rye flakes, corn meal, wheat germ, dried kelp and other natural ingredients. The manufacturers recommend that the food be mixed with fresh meat in a ratio of two parts grain to one part meat. As an alternative to fresh meat, investigate freeze-dried meat and fermented meat products, which makers claim are more nutritious and digestible for dogs.

Proper Care

by gradually introducing solid foods and decreasing the milk meals. Pups may even start themselves off on the weaning process, albeit inadvertently, if they snatch bites from their mom's food bowl.

By the time the pups are ready for new homes, they are fully weaned and eating a good puppy food. As a new owner, you may be thinking, "Great! The breeder has taken care of the hard part." Not so fast.

A puppy's first year of life is the time when all or most of his growth and development takes place. This is a delicate time, and diet plays a huge role in proper skeletal and muscular formation. Improper diet and exercise habits can lead to damaging problems that will compromise the dog's health and movement for his entire life. That being said, new owners should not worry needlessly. With the myriad types of food formulated specifically for growing pups of different-sized breeds, dog-food manufacturers have taken much of the guesswork out of feeding your puppy well. Since growth-food formulas are designed to provide the nutrition that a growing puppy needs, it is unnecessary and, in fact, can

As age is a key factor in food selection, puppies and adults do not eat the same food. Your Skye puppy will be accustomed to the food that his breeder offered at the kennel.

DIET DON'TS
- Got milk? Don't give it to your dog! Dogs cannot tolerate large quantities of cows' milk, as they do not have the enzymes to digest lactose.
- You may have heard of dog owners who add raw eggs to their dogs' food for a shiny coat or to make the food more palatable, but consumption of raw eggs too often can cause a deficiency of the vitamin biotin.
- Avoid feeding table scraps, as they will upset the balance of the dog's complete food. Additionally, fatty or highly seasoned foods can cause upset canine stomachs.
- Do not offer raw meat to your dog. Raw meat can contain parasites; it also is high in fat.
- Vitamin A toxicity in dogs can be caused by too much raw liver, especially if the dog already gets enough vitamin A in his balanced diet, which should be the case.
- Bones like chicken, pork chop and other soft bones are not suitable, as they easily splinter.

SKYE TERRIER

These Skye puppies are three weeks old and will soon start to be weaned. By the time they are eight weeks old, they should be eating a proprietary puppy food.

prove harmful to add supplements to the diet. Research has shown that too much of certain vitamin supplements and minerals predispose a dog to skeletal problems. It's by no means a case of "if a little is good, a lot is better." At every stage of your dog's life, too much or too little in the way of nutrients can be harmful, which is why a manufactured complete food is the easiest way to know that your dog is getting what he needs.

Because of a young pup's small body and accordingly small digestive system, his daily portion will be divided up into small meals throughout the day. This can mean starting off with three or more meals a day and decreasing the number of meals as the pup matures. At about 9 to 12 months, an adult diet can be fed. Eventually you can feed only one meal a day, although it is generally thought that dividing the day's food into two meals on a morning/evening schedule is healthier for the dog's digestion.

Regarding the feeding schedule, feeding the pup at the same times and in the same place each day is important for both housebreaking purposes and establishing the dog's everyday routine. As for the amount to feed, growing puppies generally need proportionately more food per body weight than their adult counter-

Proper Care

parts, but a pup should never be allowed to gain excess weight. Dogs of all ages should be kept in proper body condition, but extra weight can strain a pup's developing frame, causing skeletal problems.

Watch your pup's weight as he grows and, if the recommended amounts seem to be too much or too little for your pup, consult the vet about appropriate dietary changes. Keep in mind that treats, although small, can quickly add up throughout the day, contributing unnecessary calories. Treats are fine when used prudently; opt for dog treats specially formulated to be healthy or for nutritious snacks like small pieces of cheese or cooked chicken.

Feeding the Adult Dog

For the adult (about 9 to 12 months of age, depending on the breeder's recommendation) dog, feeding properly is about maintenance, not growth. Again, correct weight is a concern. Your dog should appear fit and should have an evident "waist." His ribs should not be protruding (a sign of being underweight), but they should be covered by only a slight layer of fat. Under normal circumstances, an adult dog can be maintained fairly easily with a high-quality nutritionally complete adult-formula food.

Factor treats into your dog's overall daily caloric intake, and avoid offering table scraps. Overweight dogs are more prone to health problems. Research has even shown that obesity takes years off a dog's life. With that in mind, resist the urge to overfeed and over-treat. Don't make unnecessary additions to your dog's diet, whether with tidbits or with extra vitamins and minerals.

The amount of food needed for proper maintenance will vary depending on the individual dog's activity level, but you will be able to tell whether the daily portions are keeping him in good shape. With the wide variety of good complete foods available, choosing what to feed is largely a matter of personal preference. Just as with the puppy, the adult dog should have consistency in his mealtimes and feeding place. In addition to a consistent routine, regular mealtimes also allow the owner to see how much his dog is eating. If the dog seems never to

---

FREE FEEDING

Many owners opt to feed their dogs the free way. That is, they serve dry kibble in a feeder, that is available to the dog all day. Arguably, this is the most convenient method of feeding an adult dog, but it may encourage the dog to become fussy about food or defensive over his bowl. Free feeding is an option only for adult dogs, not puppies.

be satisfied or, likewise, becomes uninterested in his food, the owner will know right away that something is wrong and can consult the vet.

DIETS FOR THE AGING DOG

A good rule of thumb is that once a dog has reached 75% of his expected lifespan, he has reached "senior citizen" or geriatric status. Your Skye Terrier will be considered a senior at about 8 years of age; based on his size, he has a projected lifespan of about 12 to 15 years. (The smallest breeds generally enjoy the longest lives and the largest breeds the shortest.) In Skyes, the switch to a senior diet usually takes place around eight years of age if necessary.

What does aging have to do with your dog's diet? No, he won't get a discount at the local diner's early-bird special. Yes, he will require some dietary changes to accommodate the changes that come along with increased age. One change is that the older dog's dietary needs become more similar to that of a puppy. Specifically, dogs can metabolize more protein as youngsters and seniors than in the adult-maintenance stage. Discuss with your vet whether you need to switch to a higher-protein or senior-formulated food or whether your current adult-dog food contains sufficient nutrition for the senior.

Watching the dog's weight remains essential, even more so in the senior stage. Older dogs are already more vulnerable to illness, and obesity only contributes to their susceptibility to problems. As the older dog becomes less active and, thus, exercises less, his regular portions may cause him to gain weight. At this point, you may consider decreasing his daily food intake or switching to a reduced-calorie food. As with other changes, you should consult your vet for advice.

DON'T FORGET THE WATER!

For a dog, it's always time for a drink! Regardless of what type of food he eats, there's no doubt that he needs plenty of water. Fresh cold water, in a clean bowl, should be freely available to your dog at all times. There are special circumstances, such as during puppy housebreaking, when you will want to monitor your pup's water intake so that you will be able to predict when he will need to relieve himself, but water must be available to him nonetheless. Water is essential for hydration and proper body function just as it is in humans.

You will get to know how much your dog typically drinks in a day. Of course, in the heat or if exercising vigorously, he will be more thirsty and will drink more. However, if he begins to drink noticeably more water for no apparent reason, this could signal any of various problems, and you are advised to consult your vet.

Water is the best drink for dogs. Some owners are tempted to give milk from time to time or to moisten dry food with milk, but dogs do not have the enzymes necessary to digest the lactose in milk, which is much different from the milk that nursing puppies receive. Therefore stick with clean fresh water to quench your dog's thirst, and always have it readily available to him.

EXERCISE

Exercise is important for all breeds of dog, and terriers, in general, are active, feisty creatures. No exception to the rule, the Skye will welcome the opportunity to exercise with his owner, whether this means two daily walks or a romp in the yard with a hard rubber or tennis ball.

As current health trends tell us, a sedentary lifestyle is as harmful to a dog as it is to a person. A dog is as good an excuse as any for a human to become more active. Your Skye will enjoy whatever activity you plan—a hike, a jog, a swim—anything is worth a try provided the activity does not stress the Skye's back. Brisk walks, once the puppy reaches three or four months of age, will stimulate heart rates and build muscle for both dog and owner. As the dog reaches adulthood, the speed and distance of the walks can be increased as long as they are both kept reasonable and comfortable for both of you.

> **QUENCHING HIS THIRST**
>
> Is your dog drinking more than normal and trying to lap up everything in sight? Excessive drinking has many different causes. Obvious causes for a dog's being thirstier than usual are hot weather and vigorous exercise. However, if your dog is drinking more for no apparent reason, you could have cause for concern. Serious conditions like kidney or liver disease, diabetes and various types of hormonal problems can all be indicated by excessive drinking. If you notice your dog's being excessively thirsty, contact your vet at once. Hopefully there will be a simpler explanation, but the earlier a serious problem is detected, the sooner it can be treated, with a better rate of cure.

Find ways of keeping your Skye busy. His active terrier mind will, otherwise, find other means to keep itself busy—many of which you will not condone! For instance, fetching games can be played indoors or out; these are excellent for giving your dog active play that he will enjoy. Chasing things that move comes naturally to dogs of all breeds. When your Skye runs after the ball or object, praise him for picking it up and encourage him to bring it back to you for another throw. Never go to the object and pick it up yourself, or you'll soon find that you are the one retrieving the objects rather than the dog! If you choose to play games outdoors, you must have a securely fenced-in yard and/or have the dog attached to at least a 25-foot light line for security. You want your Skye to run, but not run away!

Bear in mind that an overweight dog should never be suddenly over-exercised; instead he should be encouraged to increase exercise slowly. Not only is exercise essential to keep the dog's body fit, it is essential to his mental well-being. A bored dog will find something to do, which often manifests itself in some type of destructive behavior. In this sense, exercise is essential for the owner's mental well-being as well.

GROOMING THE SKYE TERRIER

Grooming a Skye Terrier is one of the obligations that you take on when purchasing this breed. This is a long-coated dog and his coat can become very matted if not given proper care. A matted dog can become a nuisance to have around, as he will be dirty and smelly, and if the coat is left "as is" for a long enough time, it can become a very serious health problem for the dog. This dog is like your child—keep him bathed, with his hair combed and in clean clothing, and you will have a companion whom you will want in your company.

Your Skye must be exercised on a daily basis. Once the dog is three or four months of age, a brisk walk through the neighborhood will be healthy for human and canine alike.

Proper Care   59

Start grooming your puppy as soon as he comes into your home. With a very young dog, this may only be five minutes or so a day, primarily to get the dog used to being on a grooming table and having his coat brushed. You will need the following tools: a grooming table with a rubber mat, a pinbrush, a wide-toothed comb, a knitting needle or a tail comb, sharp scissors and nail clippers.

The adult coat starts to appear at six or seven months. This is the time when you must be very diligent about your grooming, as the puppy coat is coming out and the coat can become quickly matted.

Lay your dog on the table and brush his coat with long smooth strokes, working your brush down to the skin of the dog. As your dog lies on the table, start brushing at his spine and brush toward the back of the table. This will allow you to go over every hair and to watch for any mats. Work any mats loose with your fingers or gently part them with a comb. Be sure to watch the areas where the body parts meet, such as behind the ears and the leg "pits." If you have not been diligent and have a particularly tough mat, gently slit it with a scissors. Try to keep your grooming positive for both the dog and yourself and it will be more enjoyable for both of you.

Bathe when needed, and only bathe after the coat has been brushed out and is free of any

A weekly brushing is necessary to keep your Skye's coat in good condition.

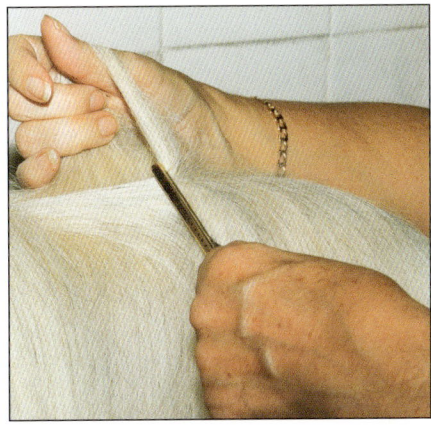

The long, outer coat should remain flat to the dog's body.

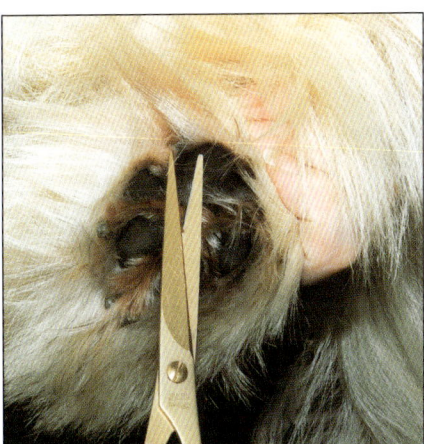

The hairs protruding from the pads on the bottom of the paws should be carefully trimmed.

mats. Bathing a matted coat will only make matters worse. Because of the long coat, let the shampoo and water flow through the coat and do not rub the coat. Use a cream rinse and follow the same procedure. To dry, use a hair dryer, pinbrush and the wide-toothed comb.

The coat part on the dog is put in with either the tail comb or with the knitting needle. Start the part at the tail and, working an inch at a time, work up the entire body, over the head and to the nose. The more often you do this, the more natural the part will become.

When grooming is completed, stand your dog up and trim all of the toenails. At this time you may also want to tidy up the feet with your scissors and perhaps trim around the penis or the vulva for cleanliness.

A weekly grooming can be an enjoyable experience for both you and your dog—quality time spent together. Remember to keep it light-hearted and positive—do not do this when you are very tired or when it is very hot, as your patience can surely be tried. And do remember that this must be a weekly procedure in order to maintain a dog that you can enjoy being around and will be proud of when walking down the street.

Bathing

Skye Terriers do not need to be bathed very frequently, but occasional bathing is helpful for healthy skin and a lustrous, elegant coat. By and large, you can keep a Skye tidy without an actual wet bath, and there are many excellent dry bath formulas on the market, but, in reality, the only way to truly clean the dog is to give it an old-fashioned B-A-T-H.

In general, dogs need to be bathed only a few times a year, possibly more often if your dog gets into something messy or if he starts to smell like a dog. Show dogs are usually bathed before

WATER SHORTAGE

No matter how well behaved your dog is, bathing is always a project! Nothing can substitute for a good warm bath, but owners do have the option of giving their dogs "dry" baths. Pet shops sell excellent products, in both powder and spray forms, designed for spot-cleaning your dog. These dry shampoos are convenient for touch-up jobs when you don't have the time to bathe your dog in the traditional way.

Muddy feet, messy behinds and smelly coats can be spot-cleaned and deodorized with a "wet-nap"-style cleaner. On those days when your dog insists on rolling in fresh goose droppings and there's no time for a bath, a spot bath can save the day. These pre-moistened wipes are also handy for other grooming needs like wiping faces, ears and eyes and freshening tails and behinds.

Proper Care

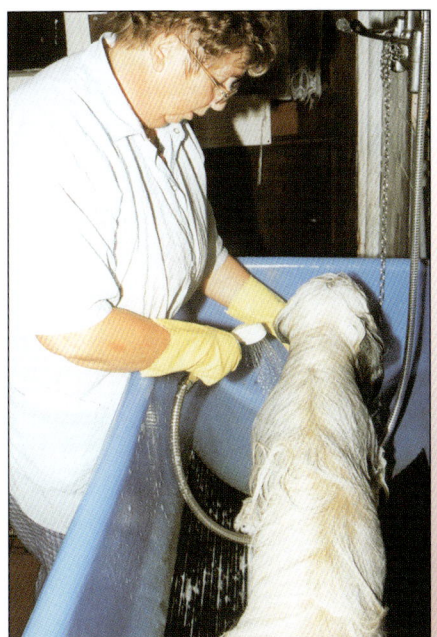 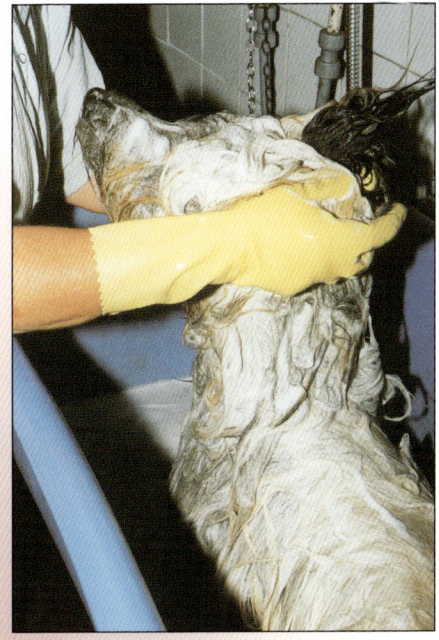

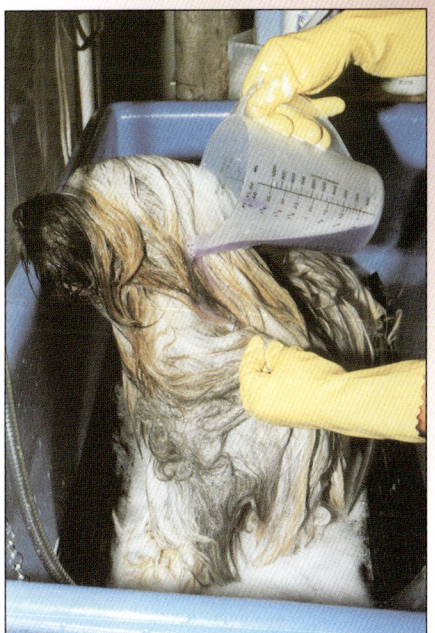 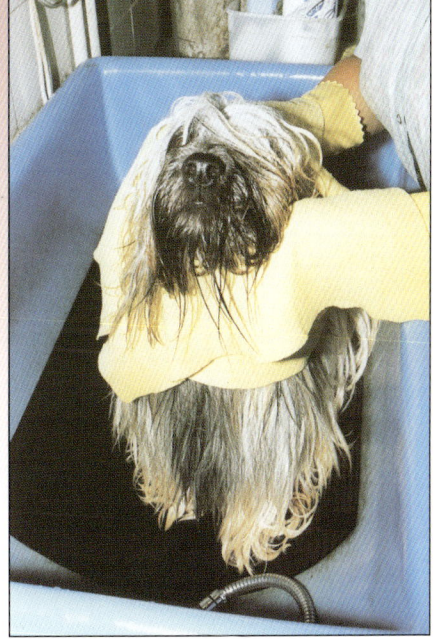

ABOVE LEFT: The Skye should be thoroughly wet down. A bath like this one is ideal for washing the Skye Terrier.
ABOVE RIGHT: As the shampoo is applied, it should be worked into the coat.
BELOW LEFT: Special shampoo for dogs should be liberally applied, always blocking the Skye's ears and eyes.
BELOW RIGHT: All of the soap must be removed from the coat before the dog can be dried.

SKYE TERRIER

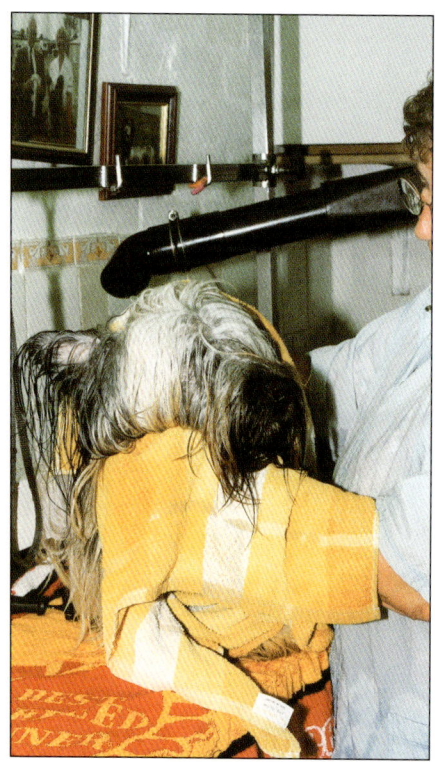

The Skye should be dried as thoroughly as possible with a very absorbent towel. A hair dryer can be used for the finishing touch.

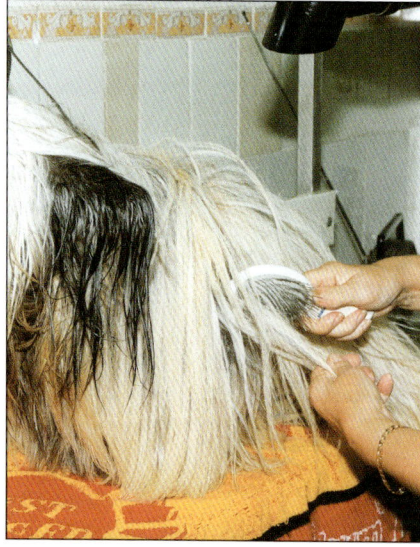

Brushing the long outer coat just before the dog is nearly completely dry will help in avoiding tangles.

every show, which could be as frequent as weekly, although this depends on the owner. Bathing too frequently can have negative effects on the skin and coat, removing natural oils and causing dryness.

If you give your dog his first bath when he is young, he will become accustomed to the process. Wrestling a dog into the tub or chasing a freshly shampooed dog who has escaped from the bath will be no fun! Most dogs don't naturally enjoy their baths, but you at least want yours to cooperate with you.

Before bathing the dog, have the items you'll need close at hand. First, decide where you will bathe the dog. You should have a tub or basin with a non-slip surface. Small dogs can even be bathed in a sink. In warm weather, some like to use a portable pool in the yard, although you'll want to make sure your dog doesn't head for the nearest dirt pile following his bath. You will also need a hose or shower spray to wet the coat thoroughly, a shampoo formulated for dogs, absorbent towels and perhaps a blow dryer. Human shampoos are too harsh for dogs' coats and will dry them out.

Before wetting the dog, give him a brush-through to remove any dead hair, dirt and mats. Make sure he is at ease in the tub and have the water at a comfortable temperature. Begin bathing by wetting the coat all the way down to the skin. Massage in the shampoo, keeping it away from his face and eyes. Rinse him thoroughly, again avoiding the eyes and ears, as you don't want to get water into the ear canals. A thorough rinsing is important, as shampoo residue is drying and itchy to the dog. After rinsing, wrap him in a towel to absorb the initial moisture. You can finish drying with either a towel or a blow dryer on low heat, held at a safe distance from the dog. You should keep the dog indoors and away from drafts until he is completely dry.

NAIL CLIPPING

Having their nails trimmed is not on many dogs' lists of favorite things to do. With this in mind, you will need to accustom your puppy to the procedure at a young age so that he will sit still (well, as still as he can) for his pedicures. Long nails can cause the dog's feet to spread, which is not good for him; likewise, long nails can hurt if they unintentionally scratch, not good for you.

Some dogs' nails are worn down naturally by regular walking on hard surfaces, so the frequency with which you clip depends on your individual dog. Look at his nails from time to time and clip as needed; a good way to know when it's time for a trim is if you hear your dog clicking as he walks across the floor.

There are several types of nail clippers and even electric nail-grinding tools made for dogs; first we'll discuss using the clipper. To start, have your clipper ready and some doggie treats on hand. You want your pup to view his nail-clipping sessions in a positive light, and what better way to convince him than with food? You may want to enlist the help of an assistant to comfort the pup and offer treats as you concentrate on the clipping itself. The guillotine-type clipper is thought of by many as the easiest type to use; the nail tip is inserted into the opening, and blades on the top and bottom snip it off in one clip.

Start by grasping the pup's paw; a little pressure on the foot pad causes the nail to extend,

A NATURAL BATH
Terrier fancier Holland Buckley wrote in 1913: "Most people wash their dogs regularly. Unless preparing a puppy for a special purpose, do not bath him at all, at least not artificially, but get him used to swimming in a pond or the river, never forgetting to give him a good gallop and a rub down afterwards. A few minutes spent each day with a comb and a dandy brush will keep the coat in tip-top condition, and the skin supple and healthy."

64 SKYE TERRIER

A non-slip grooming table serves well both during dog shows and grooming sessions.

making it easier to clip. Clip off a little at a time. If you can see the "quick," which is a blood vessel that runs through each nail, you will know how much to trim, as you do not want to cut into the quick. On that note, if you do cut the quick, which will cause bleeding, you can stem the flow of blood with a styptic pencil or other clotting agent. If you mistakenly nip the quick, do not panic or fuss, as this will cause the pup to be afraid. Simply reassure the pup, stop the bleeding and move on to the next nail. Don't be discouraged; you will become a professional canine pedicurist with practice.

You may or may not be able to see the quick, so it's best to just clip off a small bit at a time. If you see a dark dot in the center of the nail, this is the quick and your cue to stop clipping. Tell the puppy he's a "good boy" and offer a piece of treat with each nail. You can also use nail-clipping time to examine the footpads, making sure that they are not dry and cracked and that nothing has become embedded in them.

The nail grinder, the other choice, is many owners' first choice. Accustoming the puppy to the sound of the grinder and sensation of the buzz presents fewer challenges than the clipper, and there's no chance of cutting through the quick. Use the grinder on a low setting and always talk

THE MONTHLY GRIND

If your dog doesn't like the feeling of nail clippers or if you're not comfortable using them, you may wish to try an electric nail grinder. This tool has a small sandpaper disc on the end that rotates to grind the nails down. Some feel that using a grinder reduces the risk of cutting into the quick; this can be 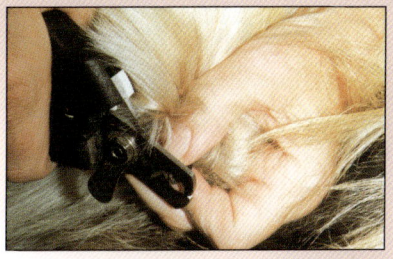 true if the tool is used properly. Usually you will be able to tell where the quick is before you get to it. A benefit of the grinder is that it creates a smooth finish on the nails so that there are no ragged edges.

Because the tool makes noise, your dog should be introduced to it before the actual grinding takes place. Turn it on and let your dog hear the noise; turn it off and let him inspect it with you holding it. Use the grinder gently, holding it firmly and progressing a little at a time until you reach the proper length. Look at the nail as you grind so that you do not go too short. Stop at any indication that you are nearing the quick. It will take a few sessions for both you and the puppy to get used to the grinder. Make sure that you don't let his hair get tangled in the grinder!

66 SKYE TERRIER

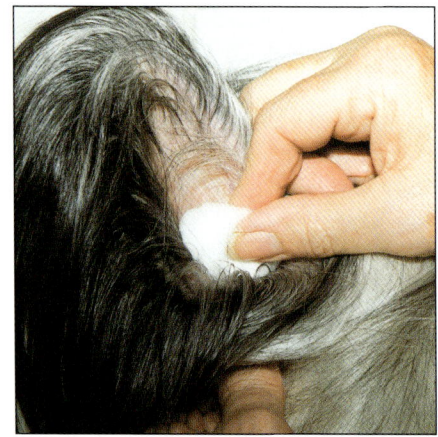

A soft wipe should cleanse the ear sufficiently when assisted by an ear cleaner, available from vets or pet shops.

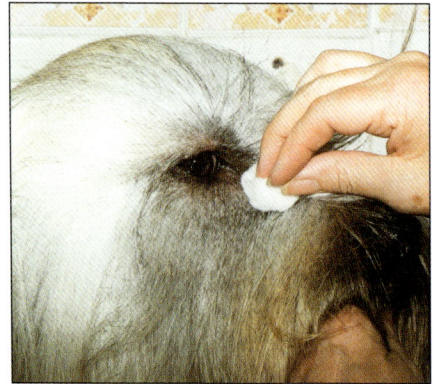

The same type of soft wipe can assist in removing tear stains around the eyes. Some pet shops sell special tear-stain removers.

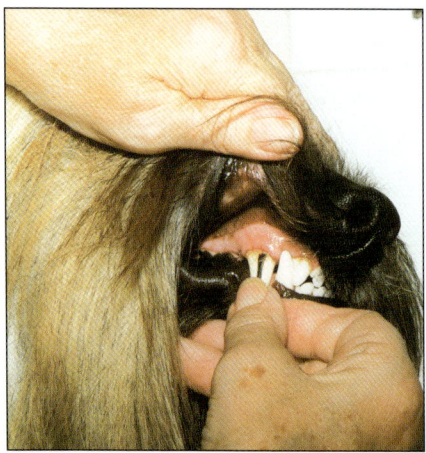

Don't forget the Skye's teeth. Brushing helps to ensure proper dental health and the desired white teeth and pink gums.

soothingly to your dog. He won't mind his salon visit, and he'll have nicely polished nails as well.

EAR CLEANING

While keeping your dog's ears clean unfortunately will not cause him to "hear" your commands any better, it will protect him from ear infection and ear-mite infestation. In addition, a dog's ears are vulnerable to waxy build-up and to collecting foreign matter from the outdoors. Look in your dog's ears regularly to ensure that they look pink, clean and otherwise healthy. Even if they look fine, an odor in the ears signals a problem and means it's time to call the vet.

A dog's ears should be cleaned regularly; once a week is suggested, and you can do this along with your regular brushing. Using a cotton ball or pad, and never probing into the ear canal, wipe the ear gently. You can use an ear-cleansing liquid or powder available from your vet or pet-supply store; alternatively, you might prefer to use homemade solutions with ingredients like one part white vinegar and one part hydrogen peroxide. Ask your vet about home remedies before you attempt to concoct something on your own.

Keep your dog's ears free of excess hair by plucking it as needed. If done gently, this will be painless for the dog. Look for wax, brown droppings (a sign of ear mites), redness or any other abnormalities. At the first sign of a problem, contact your vet so that he can prescribe an appropriate medication.

EYE CARE
During grooming sessions, pay extra attention to the condition of your dog's eyes. If the area around the eyes is soiled or if tear staining has occurred, there are various cleaning agents made especially for this purpose. Look at the dog's eyes to make sure no debris has entered; dogs with large eyes and those who spend time outdoors are especially prone to this.

The signs of an eye infection are obvious: mucus, redness, puffiness, scabs or other signs of irritation. If your dog's eyes become infected, the vet will likely prescribe an antibiotic ointment for treatment. If you notice signs of more serious problems, such as opacities in the eye, which usually indicate cataracts, consult the vet at once. Taking time to pay attention to your dog's eyes will alert you in the early stages of any problem so that you can get your dog treatment as soon as possible. You could save your dog's sight.

IDENTIFICATION AND TRAVEL

ID FOR YOUR DOG
You love your Skye Terrier and want to keep him safe. Of course you take every precaution to prevent his escaping from the yard or becoming lost or stolen. You have a sturdy high fence and you always keep your dog on lead when out and about in public places. If your dog is not properly identified, however, you are overlooking a major aspect of his safety. We hope to never be in a situation where our dog is missing, but we should practice prevention in the unfortunate case that this happens; identification

---

SCOOTING HIS BOTTOM

Here's a doggy problem that many owners tend to neglect. If your dog is scooting his rear end around the carpet, he probably is experiencing anal-sac impaction or blockage. The anal sacs are the two grape-sized glands on either side of the dog's vent. The dog cannot empty these glands, which become filled with a foul-smelling material. The dog may attempt to lick the area to relieve the pressure. He may also rub his anus on your walls, furniture or floors.

Don't neglect your dog's rear end during grooming sessions. By squeezing both sides of the anus with a soft cloth, you can express some of the material in the sacs. If the material is pasty and thick, you likely will need the assistance of a veterinarian. Vets know how to express the glands and can show you how to do it correctly without hurting the dog or spraying yourself with the unpleasant liquid.

greatly increases the chances of your dog's being returned to you.

There are several ways to identify your dog. First, the traditional dog tag should be a staple in your dog's wardrobe, attached to his everyday collar. Tags can be made of sturdy plastic and various metals and should include your contact information so that a person who finds the dog can get in touch with you right away to arrange his return. Many people today enjoy the wide range of decorative tags available, so have fun and create a tag to match your dog's personality. Of course, it is important that the tag stays on the collar, so have a secure "O" ring attachment; you also can explore the type of tag that slides right onto the collar.

In addition to the ID tag, which every dog should wear even if identified by another method, two other forms of identification have become popular: microchipping and tattooing. In microchipping, a tiny scannable chip is painlessly inserted under the dog's skin. The number is registered to you so that, if your lost dog turns up at a clinic or shelter, the chip can be scanned to retrieve your contact information.

The advantage of the microchip is that it is a permanent form of ID, but there are some factors to consider. Several different companies make microchips, and not all are compatible with the others' scanning devices. It's best to find a

Ready for the family vacation, this dynamic duo eagerly await their travel partners. The safest way to travel with dogs is in their crates (though these smiling Skyes disagree!).

Proper Care

Select a boarding kennel for your Skye before you actually need one. You might ask your vet's advice about the facilities in your area.

company with a universal microchip that can be read by scanners made by other companies as well. It won't do any good to have the dog chipped if the information cannot be retrieved. Also, not every humane society, shelter and clinic is equipped with a scanner, although more and more facilities are equipping themselves. In fact, many shelters microchip dogs that they adopt out to new homes.

Because the microchip is not visible to the eye, the dog must wear a tag that states that he is microchipped so that whoever picks him up will know to have him scanned. He of course also should have a tag with your contact information in case his chip cannot be read. Humane societies and veterinary clinics offer microchipping service, which is usually very affordable.

Though less popular than microchipping, tattooing is another permanent method of ID for dogs. Most vets perform this service, and there are also clinics that perform dog tattooing. This is also an affordable procedure and one that will not cause much discomfort for the dog. It is best to put the tattoo in a visible area, such as the ear, to deter theft. It is sad to say that there are cases of dogs' being stolen and sold to research laboratories, but such laboratories will not accept tattooed dogs.

To ensure that the tattoo is effective in aiding your dog's return to you, the tattoo number must be registered with a national organization. That way, when someone finds a tattooed dog a phone call to the registry will quickly match the dog with his owner.

TRAINING YOUR
SKYE TERRIER

BASIC TRAINING PRINCIPLES: PUPPY VS. ADULT

There's a big difference between training an adult dog and training a young puppy. With a young puppy, everything is new! At eight to ten weeks of age, he will be experiencing many things, and he has nothing with which to compare these experiences. Up to this point, he has been with his dam and littermates, not one-on-one with people except in his interactions with his breeder and visitors to the litter.

When you first bring the puppy home, he is eager to please you. This means that he accepts doing things your way. During the next couple of months, he will absorb the basis of everything he needs to know for the rest of his life. This early age is even referred to as the "sponge" stage. After that, for the next 18 months, it's up to you to reinforce good manners by building on the foundation that you've established. Once your puppy is reliable in basic commands and behavior and has reached the appropriate age, you may gradually introduce him to some of the interesting sports, games and activities available to pet owners and their dogs.

Raising your puppy is a family affair. Each member of the

THE RIGHT START

The best advice for a potential dog owner is to start with the very best puppy that money can buy. Don't shop around for a bargain in the newspaper. You're buying a companion, not a used Buick or a second-hand Maytag. The purchase price of the dog represents a very significant part of the investment, but this is indeed a very small sum compared to the expenses of maintaining the dog in good health. If you purchase a well-bred healthy and sound puppy, you will be starting right. An unhealthy puppy can cost you thousands of dollars in unnecessary veterinary expenses and, possibly, a fortune in heartbreak as well.

family must know what rules to set forth for the puppy and how to use the same one-word commands to mean exactly the same thing every time. Even if yours is a large family, one person will soon be considered by the pup to be the leader, the alpha person in his pack, the "boss" who must be obeyed. Often that highly regarded person turns out to be the one who feeds the puppy. Food ranks very high on the puppy's list of important things. That's why your puppy is rewarded with small treats along with verbal praise when he responds to you correctly. As the puppy learns to do what you want him to do, the food rewards are gradually eliminated and only the praise remains. If you were to keep up with the food treats, you could have two problems on your hands—an obese dog and a beggar.

Training begins the minute your Skye Terrier puppy steps through the doorway of your home, so don't make the mistake of putting the puppy on the floor and telling him by your actions to "Go for it! Run wild!" Even if this is your first puppy, you must act as if you know what you're doing: be the boss. An uncertain pup may be terrified to move, while a bold one will be ready to take you at your word and start plotting to destroy the house! Before you collected your puppy,

OUR CANINE KIDS
"Everything I learned about parenting, I learned from my dog." How often adults recognize that their parenting skills are mere extensions of the education they acquired while caring for their dogs. Many owners refer to their dogs as their "kids" and treat their canine companions like real members of the family. Surveys indicate that a majority of dog owners talk to their dogs regularly, celebrate their dogs' birthdays and purchase Christmas gifts for their dogs. Another survey shows that dog owners take their dogs to the veterinarian more frequently than they visit their own physicians.

you decided where his own special place would be, and that's where to put him when you first arrive home. Give him a house tour after he has investigated his area and had a nap and a bathroom "pit stop."

Never underestimate the value of play in your pup's life, the virtues of which were instilled by his dam. All training and no play will make your Skye a dull student.

It's worth mentioning here that, if you've adopted an adult dog that is completely trained to your liking, lucky you. You're off the hook! However, if that dog spent his life up to this point in a kennel, or even in a good home but without any real training, be prepared to tackle the job ahead. A dog three years of age or older with no previous training cannot be blamed for not knowing what he was never taught. While the dog is trying to understand and learn your rules, at the same time he has to unlearn many of his previously self-taught habits and general view of the world.

Working with a professional trainer will speed up your progress with an adopted adult dog. You'll need patience, too. Some new rules may be close to impossible for the dog to accept. After all, he's been successful so far by doing everything his way. (Patience again.) He may agree with your instruction for a few days and then slip back into his old ways, so you must be just as consistent and understanding in your teaching as you would be with a puppy. (More patience needed yet again!) Your dog has to learn to pay attention to your voice, your family, the daily routine, new smells, new sounds and, in some cases, even a new climate.

One of the most important things to find out about a newly adopted adult dog is his reaction to children (yours and others), strangers and your friends and how he acts upon meeting other dogs. If he was not socialized with dogs as a puppy, this could be a major problem. This does not mean that he's a "bad" dog, a vicious dog or an aggressive dog; rather, it means that he has no

CREATURES OF HABIT

Canine behaviorists and trainers aptly describe dogs as "creatures of habit," meaning that dogs respond to structure in their daily lives and welcome a routine. Do not interpret this to mean that dogs enjoy endless repetition in their training sessions. Dogs get bored just as humans do. Keep training sessions interesting and exciting. Vary the commands and the locations in which you practice. Give short breaks for play in between lessons. A bored student will never be the best performer in the class.

Training

> **SMILE WHEN YOU ORDER ME AROUND!**
> While trainers recommend practicing with your dog every day, it's perfectly acceptable to take a "mental health day" off. It's better not to train the dog on days when you're in a sour mood. Your bad attitude or lack of interest will be sensed by your dog, and he will respond accordingly. Studies show that dogs are well tuned in to their humans' emotions. Be conscious of how you use your voice when talking to your dog. Raising your voice or shouting will only erode your dog's trust in you as his trainer and master.

idea how to read another dog's body language. There's no way for him to tell whether the other dog is a friend or foe. Survival instinct takes over, telling him to attack first and ask questions later. This definitely calls for professional help and, even then, may not be a behavior that can be corrected 100% reliably (or even at all). If you have a puppy, this is why it is so very important to introduce your young puppy properly to other puppies and "dog-friendly" adult dogs.

HOUSE-TRAINING YOUR SKYE TERRIER

Dogs are tactility-oriented when it comes to house-training. In other words, they respond to the surface on which they are given approval to eliminate. The choice is yours (the dog's version is in parentheses): The lawn (including the neighbors' lawns)? A bare patch of earth under a tree (where people like to sit and relax in the summertime)? Concrete steps or patio (all sidewalks, garages and basement floors)? The curbside (watch out for cars)? A small area of crushed stone in a corner of the yard (mine!)? The latter is the best choice if you can manage it, because it will remain strictly for the dog's use and is easy to keep clean.

Do you have the time to commit to owning a Skye Terrier or two? A second dog may be a good idea if your living space, schedule and budget will permit.

SKYE TERRIER

Take note of your puppy's eating and drinking habits to determine when he will need to visit his potty area.

You can start out with paper-training indoors and switch over to an outdoor surface as the puppy matures and gains control over his need to eliminate. For the naysayers, don't worry—this won't mean that the dog will soil on every piece of newspaper lying around the house. You are training him to go outside, remember? Starting out by paper-training often is the only choice for a city dog.

WHEN YOUR PUPPY'S "GOT TO GO" Your puppy's need to relieve himself is seemingly non-stop, but signs of improvement will be seen each week. From 8 to 10 weeks old, the puppy will have to be taken outside every time he wakes up, about 10 to 15 minutes after every meal and after every period of play—all day long, from first thing in the morning until his bedtime! That's a total of ten or more trips per day to teach the puppy where it's okay to relieve himself. With that schedule in mind, you can see that house-training a young puppy is not a part-time job. It requires someone to be home all day.

If that seems overwhelming or impossible, do a little planning. For example, plan to pick up your puppy at the start of a vacation period. If you can't get home in the middle of the day, plan to hire a dog-sitter or ask a neighbor to come over to take the pup outside, feed him his lunch and then take him out again about ten or so minutes after he's eaten. Also make arrangements with that or another person to be

DAILY SCHEDULE
How many relief trips does your puppy need per day? A puppy up to the age of 14 weeks will need to go outside about 8 to 12 times per day! You will have to take the pup out any time he starts sniffing around the floor or turning in small circles, as well as after naps, meals, games and lessons or whenever he's released from his crate. Once the puppy is 14 to 22 weeks of age, he will require only 6 to 8 relief trips. At the ages of 22 to 32 weeks, the puppy will require about 5 to 7 trips. Adult dogs typically require 4 relief trips per day, in the morning, afternoon, evening and late at night.

CANINE DEVELOPMENT SCHEDULE

It is important to understand how and at what age a puppy develops into adulthood. If you are a puppy owner, consult this Canine Development Schedule to determine the stage of development your puppy is currently experiencing. This knowledge will help you as you work with the puppy in the weeks and months ahead.

Period	Age	Characteristics
First to Third	Birth to Seven Weeks	Puppy needs food, sleep and warmth and responds to simple and gentle touching. Needs mother for security and disciplining. Needs littermates for learning and interacting with other dogs. Pup learns to function within a pack and learns pack order of dominance. Begin socializing pup with adults and children for short periods. Pup begins to become aware of his environment.
Fourth	Eight to Twelve Weeks	Brain is fully developed. Pup needs socializing with outside world. Remove from mother and littermates. Needs to change from canine pack to human pack. Human dominance necessary. Fear period occurs between 8 and 12 weeks. Avoid fright and pain.
Fifth	Thirteen to Sixteen Weeks	Training and formal obedience should begin. Less association with other dogs, more with people, places, situations. Period will pass easily if you remember this is pup's change-to-adolescence time. Be firm and fair. Flight instinct prominent. Permissiveness and over-disciplining can do permanent damage. Praise for good behavior.
Juvenile	Four to Eight Months	Another fear period about seven to eight months of age. It passes quickly, but be cautious of fright and pain. Sexual maturity reached. Dominant traits established. Dog should understand sit, down, come and stay by now.

NOTE: THESE ARE APPROXIMATE TIME FRAMES. ALLOW FOR INDIVIDUAL DIFFERENCES IN PUPPIES.

your "emergency" contact if you have to stay late on the job. Remind yourself—repeatedly—that this hectic schedule improves as the puppy gets older.

HOME WITHIN A HOME
Your Skye Terrier puppy needs to be confined to one secure, puppy-proof area when no one is able to watch his every move. Generally, the kitchen is the place of choice because the floor is washable. Likewise, it's a busy family area that will accustom the pup to a variety of noises, everything from pots and pans to the telephone, blender and dishwasher. He will also be enchanted by the smell of your cooking (and will never be critical when you burn something). An exercise pen (also called an "ex-pen," a puppy version of a playpen) within the room of choice is an excellent means of confinement for a young pup. He can see out and has a certain amount of space in which to run about, but he is safe from dangerous things like electrical cords, heating units, trash baskets or open kitchen-supply cabinets. Place the pen where the puppy will not get a blast of heat or air conditioning.

In the pen, you can put a few toys, his bed (which can be his crate if the dimensions of pen and crate are compatible) and a few layers of newspaper in one small corner, just in case. A water bowl can be hung at a convenient height on the side of the ex-pen so it won't become a splashing pool for an innovative puppy. His food dish can go on the floor, next to the water bowl.

Crates are something that pet owners are at last getting used to for their dogs. Wild or domestic canines have always preferred to sleep in den-like safe spots, and

> **KIDS RULE**
> Children of 10 to 12 year of age are old enough to understand the "be kind to dumb animals" approach and will have fun training their dogs, especially to do tricks. It teaches them to be tolerant, patient and appreciative as well as to accept failure to some extent. Young children can be tyrants, making unreasonable demands of the dog and unable to cope with defeat, blaming it all on the dog. Toddlers need not apply.

that is exactly what the crate provides. How often have you seen adult dogs that choose to sleep under a table or chair even though they have full run of the house? It's the den connection.

In your "happy" voice, use the word "Crate" every time you put the pup into his den. If he's new to a crate, toss in a small biscuit for him to chase the first few times. At night, after he's been outside, he should sleep in his crate. The crate may be kept in his designated area at night or, if you want to be sure to hear those wake-up yips in the morning, put the crate in a corner of your bedroom. However, don't

Train your Skye Terrier to always use the same area of the property for bathroom duties. This makes for more convenient toileting as well as clean up.

> **POTTY COMMAND**
> Most dogs love to please their masters; there are no bounds to what dogs will do to make their owners happy. The potty command is a good example of this theory. If toileting on command makes the master happy, then more power to him. Puppies will obligingly piddle if it really makes their keepers smile. Some owners can be creative about which word they will use to command their dogs to relieve themselves. Some popular choices are "Potty," "Tinkle," "Piddle," "Let's go," "Hurry up" and "Toilet." Give the command every time your puppy goes into position, and the puppy will begin to associate his business with the command.

make any response whatsoever to whining or crying. If he's completely ignored, he'll settle down and get to sleep.

Good bedding for a young puppy is an old folded bath towel or an old blanket, something that is easily washable and disposable if necessary ("accidents" will happen!). Never put newspaper in the puppy's crate. Also those old ideas about adding a clock to replace his mother's heartbeat or a hot-water bottle to replace her warmth, are just that—old ideas. The clock could drive the puppy nuts, and the hot-water bottle could end up as a very soggy waterbed! An extremely good breeder would have introduced your puppy to the crate by letting two pups sleep together for a couple of nights, followed by several nights alone. How thankful you will be if you found that breeder!

SKYE TERRIER

Learn to read the signs that your Skye puppy is ready "to go." Puppies try hard to relay their needs to their people.

Safe toys in the pup's crate or area will keep him occupied, but monitor their condition closely. Discard any toys that show signs of being chewed to bits. Squeaky parts, bits of stuffing or plastic or any other small pieces can cause intestinal blockage or possibly choking if ingested.

PROGRESSING WITH POTTY-TRAINING
After you've taken your puppy out and he has relieved himself in the area you've selected, he can have some free time with the family as long as there is someone responsible for watching him. That doesn't mean just someone in the same room who is watching TV or busy on the computer, but one person who is doing nothing other than keeping an eye on the pup, playing with him on the floor and helping him understand his position in the pack.

This first taste of freedom will let you begin to set the house rules. If you don't want the dog on the furniture, now is the time to prevent his first attempts to jump up onto the couch. The word to use in this case is "Off," not "Down." "Down" is the word you will use to teach the down position, which is something entirely different.

SOMEBODY TO BLAME
House-training a puppy can be frustrating for the puppy and the owner alike. The puppy does not instinctively understand the difference between defecating on the pavement outside and on the ceramic tile in the kitchen. He is confused and frightened by his human's exuberant reactions to his natural urges. The owner, arguably the more intelligent of the duo, is also frustrated that he cannot convince his puppy to obey his commands and instructions.

In frustration, the owner may struggle with the temptation to discipline the puppy, scold him or even strike him on the rear end. Harsh corrections are unnecessary and inappropriate, serving to defeat your purpose in gaining your puppy's trust and respect. Don't blame your nine-week-old puppy. Blame yourself for not being 100% consistent in the puppy's lessons and routine. The lesson here is simple: try harder and your puppy will succeed.

Training

Most corrections at this stage come in the form of simply distracting the puppy. Instead of telling him "No" for "Don't chew the carpet," distract the chomping puppy with a toy and he'll forget about the carpet.

As you are playing with the pup, do not forget to watch him closely and pay attention to his body language. Whenever you see him begin to circle or sniff, take the puppy outside to relieve himself. If you are paper-training, put him back into his confined area on the newspapers. In either case, praise him as he eliminates while he actually is in the act of relieving himself. Three seconds after he has finished is too late! You'll be praising him for running toward you, picking up a toy or whatever he may be doing at that moment, and that's not what you want to be praising him for. Timing is a vital tool in all dog training. Use it.

Remove soiled newspapers immediately and replace them with clean ones. You may want to take a small piece of soiled paper and place it in the middle of the new clean papers, as the scent will attract him to that spot when it's time to go again. That scent attraction is why it's so important to clean up any messes made in the house by using a product specially made to eliminate the odor of dog urine and droppings. Regular household cleansers won't do the trick. Pet shops sell the best pet deodorizers. Invest in the largest container you can find.

Scent attraction eventually will lead your pup to his chosen spot outdoors; this is the basis of outdoor training. When you take your puppy outside to relieve himself, use a one-word command such as "Outside" or "Go-potty" (that's one word to the puppy!) as you attach his leash. Then lead him to his spot. Now comes the hard part—hard for you, that is. Just stand there until he urinates and defecates. Move him a few feet in one direction or another if he's just sitting there looking at you, but remember that this is neither playtime

> **TIDY BOY**
> Clean by nature, dogs do not like to soil their dens, which in effect are their crates or sleeping quarters. Unless not feeling well, dogs will not defecate or urinate in their crates. Crate training capitalizes on the dog's natural desire to keep his den clean. Be conscientious about giving the puppy as many opportunities to relieve himself outdoors as possible. Reward the puppy for correct behavior. Praise him and pat him whenever he "goes" in the correct location. Even the tidiest of puppies can have potty accidents, so be patient and dedicate more energy to helping your puppy achieve a clean lifestyle.

> **KEEP IT SIMPLE—AND FUN**
> Keep your lessons simple, interesting and user-friendly. Fun breaks help you both. Spend two minutes or ten teaching your puppy, but practice only as long as your dog enjoys what he's doing and is focused on pleasing you. If he's bored or distracted, stop the training session after any correct response (always end on a high note!). After a few minutes of playtime, you can go back to "hitting the books."

nor time for a walk. This is strictly a business trip! Then, as he circles and squats (remember your timing!), give him a quiet "Good dog" as praise. If you start to jump for joy, ecstatic over his performance, he'll do one of two things: either he will stop midstream, as it were, or he'll do it again for you—in the house—and expect you to be just as delighted!

Give him five minutes or so and, if he doesn't go in that time, take him back indoors to his confined area and try again in another ten minutes, or immediately if you see him sniffing and circling. By careful observation, you'll soon work out a successful schedule.

Accidents, by the way, are just that—accidents. Clean them up quickly and thoroughly, without comment, after the puppy has been taken outside to finish his business and then put back into his area or crate. If you witness an accident in progress, say "No!" in a stern voice and get the pup outdoors immediately. No punishment is needed. You and your puppy are just learning each other's language, and sometimes it's easy to miss a puppy's message. Chalk it up to experience and watch more closely from now on.

KEEPING THE PACK ORDERLY
Discipline is a form of training that brings order to life. For example, military discipline is what allows the soldiers in an army to work as one. Discipline is a form of teaching and, in dogs, is the basis of how the successful pack operates. Each member knows his place in the pack and all respect the leader, or alpha dog. It is essential for your puppy that you establish this type of relationship, with you as the alpha, or leader. It is a form of social coexistence that all canines recognize and accept. Discipline, therefore, is never to be confused with punishment. When you teach your puppy how you want him to behave and he behaves properly and you praise him for it, you are disciplining him with a form of positive reinforcement.

For a dog, rewards come in the form of praise, a smile, a cheerful tone of voice, a few friendly pats or a rub of the ears. Rewards are also small food treats. Obviously, that does not mean bits of regular dog food. Instead, treats are very small bits of special things like cheese or pieces of soft dog treats. The idea is to reward the dog with something very small that he can taste and swallow, providing instant positive reinforcement. If he has to take time to chew the treat, he will have forgotten what he did to earn it by the time he is finished.

Your puppy should never be physically punished. The displeasure shown on your face and in your voice is sufficient to signal to the pup that he has done something wrong. He wants to please everyone higher up on the social ladder, especially his leader, so a scowl and harsh voice will take care of the error. Growling out the word "Shame!" when the pup is caught in the act of doing something wrong is better than the repetitive "No." Some dogs hear "No" so often that they begin to think it's their name! By the way, do not use the dog's name when you're correcting him. His name is reserved to get his attention for something pleasant about to take place.

There are punishments that have nothing to do with you. For example, your dog may think that chasing cats is one reason for his existence. You can try to stop it as much as you like but without success, because it's such fun for the dog. But one good hissing, spitting swipe of a cat's claws across the dog's nose will put an end to the game forever. Intervene only when your dog's eyeball is seriously at risk. Cat scratches can cause permanent damage to an innocent but annoying puppy.

PUPPY KINDERGARTEN

COLLAR AND LEASH
Before you begin your Skye Terrier puppy's education, he must be used to his collar and leash. Choose a collar for your puppy that is secure but not heavy or bulky. He won't enjoy training if he's uncomfortable. A flat buckle collar is fine for

> **BASIC PRINCIPLES OF DOG TRAINING**
> 1. Start training early. A young puppy is ready, willing and able.
> 2. Timing is your all-important tool. Praise at the exact time that the dog responds correctly. Pay close attention.
> 3. Patience is almost as important as timing!
> 4. Repeat! The same word has to mean the same thing every time.
> 5. In the beginning, praise all correct behavior verbally, along with treats and petting.

everyday wear and for initial puppy training. For older dogs, there are several types of training collars such as the martingale, which is a double loop that tightens slightly around the neck, or the head collar, which is similar to a horse's halter. Do not use a chain choke collar unless you have been specifically shown how to put it on and how to use it. You may not be disposed to use a chain choke collar even if your breeder has told you that it's suitable for your Skye Terrier.

A lightweight 6-foot woven cotton or nylon training leash is preferred by most trainers because it is easy to fold up in your hand and comfortable to hold because there is a certain amount of give to it. There are lessons where the dog will start off 6 feet away from you at the end of the leash. The leash used to take the puppy outside to relieve himself is shorter because you don't want him to roam away from his area. The shorter leash will also be the one to use when you walk the puppy.

If you've been wise enough to enroll in a puppy kindergarten training class, suggestions will be made as to the best collar and leash for your young puppy. I say "wise" because your puppy will be in a class with puppies in his age range (up to five months old) of all breeds and sizes. It's the perfect way for him to learn the right way (and the wrong way) to interact with other dogs as well as their people. You cannot teach your puppy how to interpret another dog's sign language. For a first-time puppy owner, these socialization classes are invaluable. For experienced dog owners, they are a real boon to further training.

> **LEADER OF THE PACK**
> Canines are pack animals. They live according to pack rules, and every pack has only one leader. Guess what? That's you! To establish your position of authority, lay down the rules and be fair and good-natured in all your dealings with your dog. He will consider young children as his littermates, but the one who trains him, who feeds him, who grooms him, who expects him to come into line, that's his leader. And he who leads must be obeyed.

Training

> **TEACHER'S PET**
>
> Dogs are individuals, not robots, with many traits basic to their breed. Some, bred to work alone, are independent thinkers; others rely on you to call the shots. If you have enrolled in a training class, your instructor can offer alternative methods of training based on your individual dog's instincts and personality. You may benefit from using a different type of collar or switching to a class with different kinds of dogs.

ATTENTION

You've been using the dog's name since the minute you collected him from the breeder, so you should be able to get his attention by saying his name—with a big smile and in an excited tone of voice. His response will be the puppy equivalent of "Here I am! What are we going to do?" Your immediate response (if you haven't guessed by now) is "Good dog." Rewarding him at the moment he pays attention to you teaches him the proper way to respond when he hears his name.

EXERCISES FOR A BASIC CANINE EDUCATION

THE SIT EXERCISE

There are several ways to teach the puppy to sit. The first one is to catch him whenever he is about to sit and, as his backside nears the floor, say "Sit, good dog!" That's positive reinforcement and, if your timing is sharp, he will learn that what he's doing at that second is connected to your saying "Sit" and that you think he's clever for doing it.

Another method is to start with the puppy on his leash in front of you. Show him a treat in the palm of your right hand. Bring your hand up under his nose and, almost in slow motion, move your hand up and back so his nose goes up in the air and his head tilts back as he follows the treat in your hand. At that point, he will have to either sit or fall over, so as his back legs buckle under, say "Sit, good dog," and then give him the treat and lots of praise. You may have to begin with your hand lightly running up his chest, actually lifting his chin up until he sits. Some (usually older) dogs require

For the Skye Terrier, the sit position is not as natural as it is for most other dogs. A little pressure on your Skye's rear will reinforce what is expected in the sit exercise.

gentle pressure on their hindquarters with the left hand, in which case the dog should be on your left side. Puppies generally do not appreciate this physical dominance.

After a few times, you should be able to show the dog a treat in the open palm of your hand, raise your hand waist-high as you say "Sit" and have him sit. You thereby will have taught him two things at the same time. Both the verbal command and the motion of the hand are signals for the sit. Your puppy is watching you almost more than he is listening to you, so what you do is just as important as what you say.

Don't save any of these drills only for training sessions. Use them as much as possible at odd times during a normal day. The dog should always sit before being given his food dish. He should sit to let you go through a doorway first, when the doorbell rings or when you stop to speak to someone on the street.

THE DOWN EXERCISE

Before beginning to teach the down command, you must consider how the dog feels about this exercise. To him, "down" is a submissive position. Being flat on the floor with you standing over him is not his idea of fun. It's up to you to let him know that, while it may not be fun, the reward of your approval is worth his effort.

Start with the puppy on your left side in a sit position. Hold the leash right above his collar in your left hand. Have an extra-special treat, such as a small piece of cooked chicken or hot dog, in your right hand. Place it at the end of the pup's nose and steadily move your hand down and forward along the ground. Hold the leash to prevent a sudden lunge for the food. As the puppy

> **DOWN**
> "Down" is a harsh-sounding word and a submissive posture in dog body language, thus presenting two obstacles in teaching the down command. When the dog is about to flop down on his own, tell him "Good down." Pups that are not good about being handled learn better by having food lowered in front of them. A dog that trusts you can be gently guided into position. When you give the command "Down," be sure to say it sweetly!

goes into the down position, say "Down" very gently.

The difficulty with this exercise is twofold: it's both the submissive aspect and the fact that most people say the word "Down" as if they were drill sergeants in charge of recruits! So issue the command sweetly, give him the treat and have the pup maintain the down position for several seconds. If he tries to get up immediately, place your hands on his shoulders and press down gently, giving him a very quiet "Good dog." As you progress with this lesson, increase the "down time" until he will hold it until you say "Okay" (his cue for release). Practice this one in the house at various times throughout the day.

By increasing the length of time during which the dog must maintain the down position, you'll find many uses for it. For example, he can lie at your feet in the vet's office or anywhere that both of you have to wait, when you are on the phone, while the family is eating and so forth. If you progress to training for competitive obedience, he'll already be all set for the exercise called the "long down."

The Stay Exercise

You can teach your Skye Terrier to stay in the sit, down and stand positions. To teach the sit/stay, have the dog sit on your left side.

DON'T STRESS ME OUT

Your dog doesn't have to deal with paying the bills, the daily commute, PTA meetings and the like, but, believe it or not, there's a lot of stress in a dog's world. Stress can be caused by the owner's impatient demeanor and his angry or harsh corrections. If your dog cringes when you reach for his training collar, he's stressed. An older dog is sometimes stressed out when he goes to a new home. No matter what the cause, put off all training until he's over it. If he's going through a fear period—shying away from people, trembling when spoken to, avoiding eye contact or hiding under furniture—wait to resume training. Naturally you'd also postpone your lessons if the dog were sick, and the same goes for you. Show some compassion.

Hold the leash at waist level in your left hand and let the dog know that you have a treat in your

> **FEAR AGGRESSION**
>
> Of the several types of aggression, the one brought on by fear is the most difficult for people to comprehend and to deal with. Aggression to protect food, or any object the dog perceives as his, is more easily understood. Fear aggression is quite different. The dog shows fear, generally for no apparent reason. He backs off, cowers or hides under the bed. If he's on lead, he will hide behind your leg and lash out unexpectedly. No matter how you approach him, he will bite. A fear-biter attacks with great speed and instantly retreats. Don't shout at him or go near him. Don't coddle, sympathize or try to protect him. To him, that's a reward. As with other forms of aggression, get professional help.

closed right hand. Step forward on your right foot as you say "Stay." Immediately turn and stand directly in front of the dog, keeping your right hand up high so he'll keep his eye on the treat hand and maintain the sit position for a count of five. Return to your original position and offer the reward.

Increase the length of the sit/stay each time until the dog can hold it for at least 30 seconds without moving. After about a week of success, move out on your right foot and take two steps before turning to face the dog. Give the "Stay" hand signal (left palm back toward the dog's head) as you leave. He gets the treat when you return and he holds the sit/stay. Increase the distance that you walk away from him before turning until you reach the length of your training leash. But don't rush it! Go back to the beginning if he moves before he should. No matter what the lesson, never be upset by having to back up for a few days. The repetition and practice are what will make your dog reliable in these commands. It won't do any good to move on to something more difficult if the command is not mastered at the easier levels. Above all, even if you do get frustrated, never let your puppy know! Always keep a positive, upbeat attitude during training, which will transmit to your dog for positive results.

The down/stay is taught in the same way once the dog is completely reliable and steady with the down command. Again, don't rush it. With the dog in the down position on your left side, step out on your right foot as you say "Stay." Return by walking around in back of the dog and into your original position. While you are training, it's okay to murmur something like "Hold on" to encourage him to stay put. When the dog will stay without moving when you are at a distance of 3 or 4 feet, begin to increase the length of time before you return. Be sure he holds the down on your return until you say "Okay." At that point, he gets his treat—just so he'll remember for next time that it's not over until it's over.

THE COME EXERCISE

No command is more important to the safety of your Skye Terrier than "Come." It is what you should say every single time you see the puppy running toward you: "Chuckles, come! Good dog." During playtime, run a few feet away from the puppy and turn and tell him to "Come" as he is already running to you. You can go so far as to teach your puppy two things at once if you squat down and hold out your arms. As the pup gets close to you and you're saying "Good dog," bring your right arm in about waist high. Now he's also learning the hand signal, an excellent device should you be on the phone when you need to get him to come to you! You'll also both be one step ahead when you enter obedience classes.

When the puppy responds to your well-timed "Come," try it with the puppy on the training leash. This time, catch him off-guard, while he's sniffing a leaf or watching a bird: "Chuckles, come!" You may have to pause for a split second after his name to be sure you have his attention. If the puppy shows any sign of confusion, give the leash a mild jerk and take a couple of steps backward. Do not repeat the command. In this case, you should say "Good come" as he reaches you.

That's the number-one rule of training. Each command word is given just once. Anything more is nagging. You'll also notice that all commands are one word only. Even when they are actually two words, you say them as one.

Never call the dog to come to you—with or without his name—if you are angry or intend to correct him for some misbehavior.

TIPS FOR TRAINING AND SAFETY

1. Whether on or off leash, practice only in a fenced area.
2. Remove the training collar when the training session is over.
3. Don't try to break up a dogfight.
4. "Come," "Leave it" and "Wait" are safety commands.
5. The dog belongs in a crate or behind a barrier when riding in the car.
6. Don't ignore the dog's first sign of aggression. Aggression only gets worse, so take it seriously.
7. Keep the faces of children and dogs separated.
8. Pay attention to what the dog is chewing.
9. Keep the vet's number near your phone.
10. "Okay" is a useful release command.

LET'S GO!
Many people use "Let's go" instead of "Heel" when teaching their dogs to behave on lead. It sounds more like fun! When beginning to teach the heel, whatever command you use, always step off on your left foot. That's the one next to the dog, who is on your left side, in case you've forgotten. Keep a loose leash. When the dog pulls ahead, stop, bring him back and begin again. Use treats to guide him around turns.

When correcting the pup, you go to him. Your dog must always connect "Come" with something pleasant and with your approval; then you can rely on his response.

Puppies, like children, have notoriously short attention spans, so don't overdo it with any of the training. Keep each lesson short. Break it up with a quick run around the yard or a ball toss, repeat the lesson and quit as soon as the pup gets it right. That way, you will always end with a "Good dog."

Life isn't perfect and neither are puppies. A time will come, often around ten months of age, when he'll become "selectively deaf" or choose to "forget" his name. He may respond by wagging his tail (and even seeming to smile at you) with a look that says "Make me!" Laugh, throw his favorite toy and skip the lesson you had planned. Pups will be pups!

THE HEEL EXERCISE
The second most important command to teach, after the come, is the heel. When you are walking your growing puppy, you need to be in control. Besides, it looks terrible to be pulled and yanked down the street, and it's not much fun either. Your eight- to ten-week-old puppy will probably follow you everywhere, but that's his natural instinct, not your control over the situation. However, any time he does follow you, you can say "Heel" and be ahead of the game, as he will learn to associate this command with the action of following you before you even begin teaching him to heel.

There is a very precise, almost military, procedure for teaching your dog to heel. As with all other obedience training, begin with the dog on your left side. He will be in a very nice sit and you will have the training leash across your chest. Hold the loop and folded leash in your right hand. Pick up the slack leash above the dog in your left hand and hold it loosely at your side. Step out on your left foot as you say "Heel." If the puppy does not move, give a gentle tug or pat your left leg to get him started. If he surges ahead of you, stop and pull him back gently until he is at your side. Tell him to sit and begin again.

Walk a few steps and stop while the puppy is correctly beside you. Tell him to sit and give mild verbal praise. (More enthusiastic praise will encourage him to think the lesson is over.) Repeat the lesson, increasing the number of steps you take only as long as the dog is heeling nicely beside you. When you end the lesson, have him hold the sit, then give him the "Okay" to let him know that this is the end of the lesson. Praise him so that he knows he did a good job.

The cure for excessive pulling (a common problem) is to stop when the dog is no more than 2 or 3 feet ahead of you. Guide him back into position and begin again. With a really determined puller, try switching to a head collar. This will automatically turn the pup's head toward you so you can bring him back easily to the heel position. Give quiet, reassuring praise every time the leash goes slack and he's staying with you.

Staying and heeling can take a lot out of a dog, so provide playtime and free-running exercise to shake off the stress when the lessons are over. You don't want him to associate training with all work and no fun.

TAPERING OFF TIDBITS
Your dog has been watching you—and the hand that treats—throughout all of his lessons, and now it's time to break the treat habit. Begin by giving him treats at the end of each lesson only. Then start to give a treat after the end of only some of the lessons.

Perhaps the most important command a show dog must master is the heel. To exhibit the proper gait in the show ring, the dog must keep pace at the owner's side without pulling ahead or lagging behind.

In show rings and homes around the world, Skye Terriers are seen more frequently and in greater numbers each year.

At the end of every lesson, as well as during the lessons, be consistent with the praise. Your pup now doesn't know whether he'll get a treat or not, but he should keep performing well just in case! Finally, you will stop giving treat rewards entirely. Save them for something brand-new that you want to teach him. Keep up the praise and you'll always have a "good dog."

OBEDIENCE CLASSES
The advantages of an obedience class are that your dog will have to learn amid the distractions of other people and dogs and that your mistakes will be quickly corrected by the trainer. Teaching your dog along with a qualified instructor and other handlers who may have more dog experience than you is another plus of the class environment. The instructor and other handlers can help you to find the most efficient way of teaching your dog a command or exercise. It's often easier to learn by other people's mistakes than your own. You will also learn all of the requirements for competitive obedience trials, in which you can earn titles and go on to advanced jumping and retrieving exercises, which are fun for many dogs. Obedience classes build the foundation needed for many other canine activities (in which we humans are allowed to participate, too!).

TRAINING FOR OTHER ACTIVITIES
Once your dog has basic obedience under his collar and is 12 months of age, you can enter the world of agility training. Dogs think agility is pure fun, like being turned loose in an amusement park full of obstacles! In addition to agility, there are

hunting activities for sporting dogs, lure-coursing events for sighthounds, go-to-ground events for terriers, racing for the Nordic sled dogs, herding trials for the shepherd breeds and tracking, which is open to all "nosey" dogs (which would include all dogs!). For those who like to volunteer,

Don't let the short legs fool you, as this mighty terrier is quite capable of doing what is asked of him.

there is the wonderful feeling of owning a therapy dog and visiting hospices, nursing homes and veterans' homes to bring smiles, comfort and companionship to those who live there.

Skye Terriers can also participate in earthdog trials, designed specifically for terriers (and Dachshunds) and tracking events. Investigate these with your local Skye Terrier club.

Around the house, your Skye Terrier can be taught to do some simple chores. You might teach him to carry a basket of household items or to fetch the morning newspaper. The kids can teach the dog all kinds of tricks, from playing hide-and-seek to balancing a biscuit on his nose. A family dog is what rounds out the family. Everything he does beyond sitting in your lap or gazing lovingly at you represents the bonus of owning a dog.

RIGHT CLICK ON YOUR DOG

With three clicks, the dolphin jumps through the hoop. Wouldn't it be nice to have a dog who could obey wordless commands that easily? Clicker training actually was developed by dolphin trainers and today is used on dogs with great success. You can buy a clicker at a pet shop or pet-supply outlet, and then you'll be off and clicking.

You can click your dog into learning new commands, shaping or conditioning his behavior and solving bad habits. The clicker, used in conjunction with a treat, is an extension of positive reinforcement. The dog begins to recognize your happy clicking and will learn what it takes to be a "good dog." The dog is conditioned to follow your hand with the clicker, just as he would follow your hand with a treat. To discourage the dog from inappropriate behavior (like jumping up or barking), you can use the clicker to set a timeframe and then click and reward the dog once he's waited the allotted time without jumping up or barking.

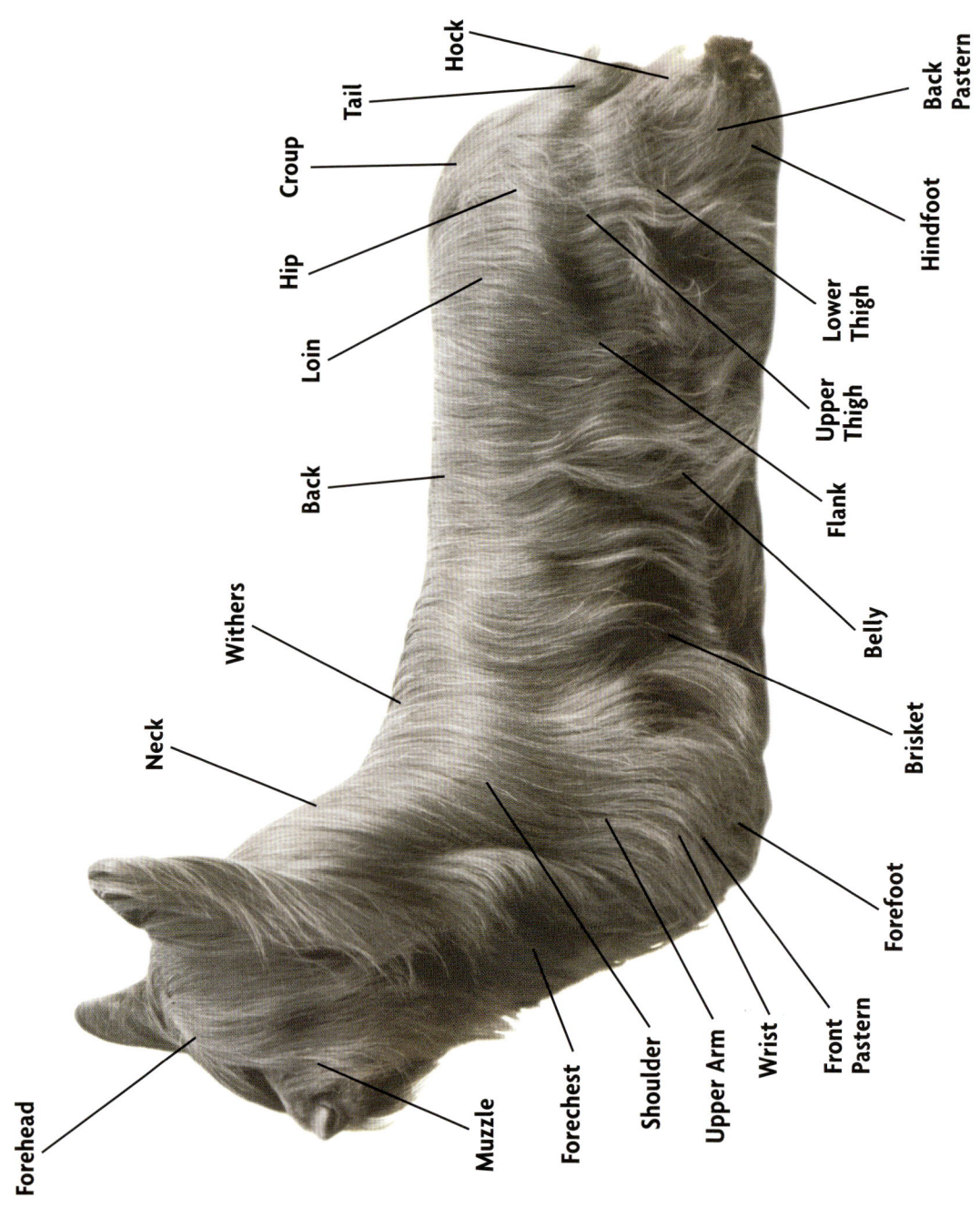

PHYSICAL STRUCTURE OF THE SKYE TERRIER

HEALTHCARE OF YOUR
SKYE TERRIER

By Lowell Ackerman DVM, DACVD

HEALTHCARE FOR A LIFETIME
When you own a dog, you become his healthcare advocate over his entire lifespan, as well as being the one to shoulder the financial burden of such care. Accordingly, it is worthwhile to focus on prevention rather than treatment, as you and your pet will both be happier.

Of course, the best place to have begun your program of preventive healthcare is with the initial purchase or adoption of your dog. There is no way of guaranteeing that your new furry friend is free of medical problems, but there are some things you can do to improve your odds. You certainly should have done adequate research into the Skye Terrier and have selected your puppy carefully rather than buying on impulse. Health issues aside, a large number of pet abandonment and relinquishment cases arise from a mismatch between pet needs and owner expectations. This is entirely preventable with appropriate planning and finding a good breeder.

Regarding healthcare issues specifically, it is very difficult to make blanket statements about where to acquire a problem-free pet, but, again, a reputable breeder is your best bet. In an ideal situation you have the opportunity to see both parents, get references from other owners of the breeder's pups and see genetic-testing documentation for several generations of the litter's ancestors. At the very least, you must thoroughly investigate the Skye Terrier and the problems inherent in that breed, as well as the genetic testing available to screen for those problems. Genetic testing offers some important benefits, but testing is available for only a few disorders in a relatively small number of breeds and is not available for some of the most common genetic diseases, such as hip dysplasia, cataracts, epilepsy, cardiomyopathy, etc. This area of research is indeed exciting and increasingly important, and advances will continue to be made each year. In fact, recent research has shown that there is an equivalent dog gene for 75% of known human genes, so research done in either species is likely to benefit the other.

We've also discussed that evaluating the behavioral nature

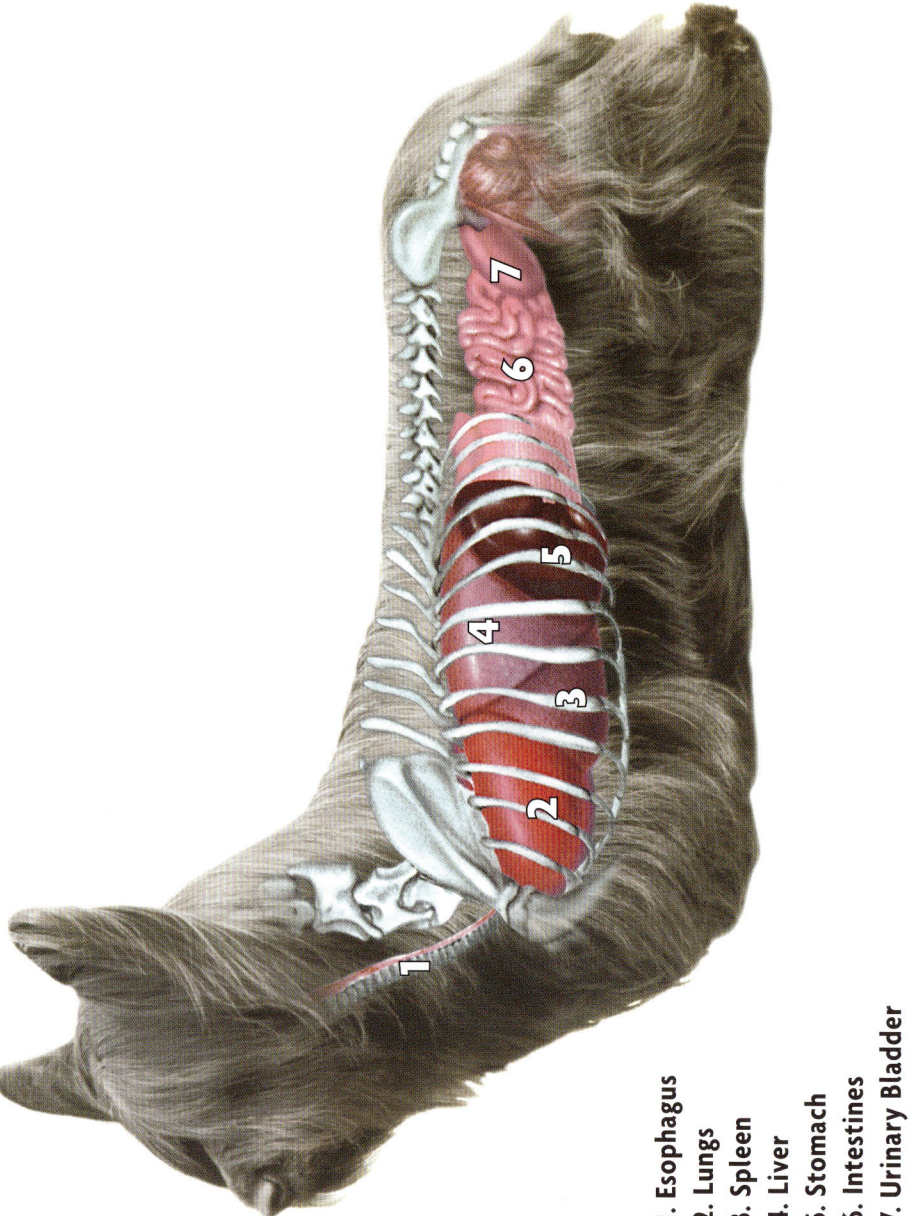

INTERNAL ORGANS OF THE SKYE TERRIER

1. Esophagus
2. Lungs
3. Spleen
4. Liver
5. Stomach
6. Intestines
7. Urinary Bladder

Healthcare

of your Skye Terrier and that of his immediate family members is an important part of the selection process that cannot be overemphasized. It is sometimes difficult to evaluate temperament in puppies because certain behavioral tendencies, such as some forms of aggression, may not be immediately evident. More dogs are euthanized each year for behavioral reasons than for all medical conditions combined, so it is critical to take temperament issues seriously. Start with a well-balanced, friendly companion and put the time and effort into proper socialization, and you will both be rewarded with a lifelong, valued relationship.

Assuming that you have started off with a pup from healthy, sound stock, you then become responsible for helping your veterinarian keep your pet healthy. Some crucial things happen before you even bring your puppy home. Parasite control typically begins at two weeks of age, and vaccinations typically begin at six to eight weeks of age. A pre-pubertal evaluation is typically scheduled for about six months of age. At this time, a dental evaluation is done (since the adult teeth are now in), heartworm prevention is started and neutering or spaying is most commonly done.

It is critical to commence regular dental care at home if you have not already done so. It may not sound very important, but most dogs have active periodontal disease by four years of age if they don't have their teeth cleaned regularly at home, not just at their veterinary exams. Dental problems lead to more than just bad "doggy breath." Gum disease can have very serious medical consequences. If you start brushing your dog's teeth and using antiseptic rinses from a young age, your dog will be accustomed to it and will not resist. The results will be healthy dentition, which your pet will need to enjoy a long, healthy life.

Most dogs are considered adults at a year of age, although some larger breeds still have some filling out to do up to about two or so years old. Even individual dogs within each breed have different healthcare requirements, so work with your veterinarian to determine what will be needed and what your role should be. This doctor-client relationship is important, because as vaccination guidelines change, there may not be an annual "vaccine visit" scheduled. You must make sure that you see your veterinarian at least annually, even if no vaccines are due, because this is the best opportunity to coordinate healthcare activities and to make sure that no medical issues creep by unaddressed.

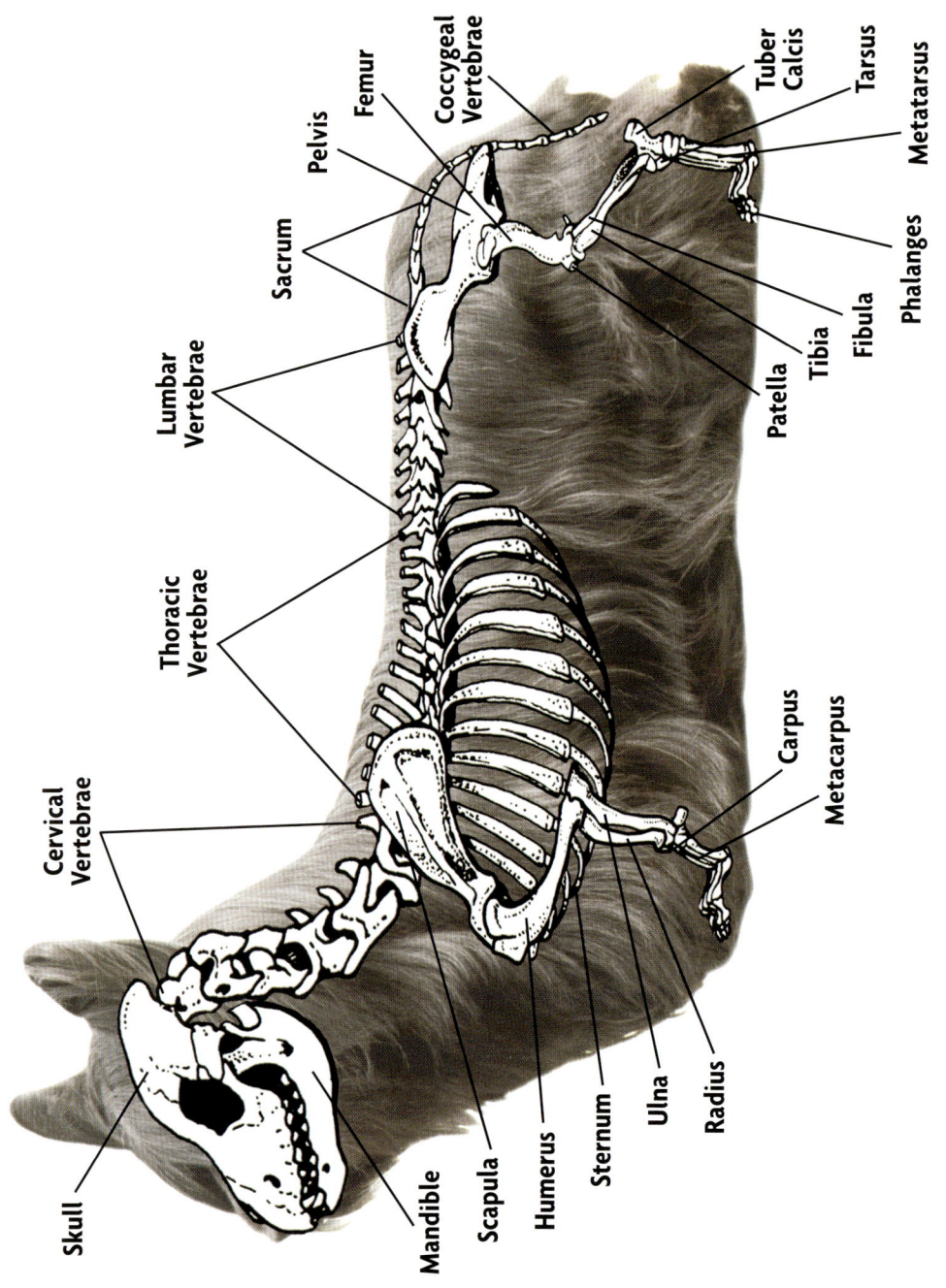

SKELETAL STRUCTURE OF THE SKYE TERRIER

Healthcare

When your Skye Terrier reaches three-quarters of his anticipated lifespan, he is considered a "senior" and likely requires some special care. In general, if you've been taking great care of your canine companion throughout his formative and adult years, the transition to senior status should be a smooth one. Age is not a disease, and as long as everything is functioning as it should, there is no reason why most of late adulthood should not be rewarding for both you and your pet. This is especially true if you have tended to the details, such as regular veterinary visits, proper dental care, excellent nutrition and management of bone and joint issues.

At this stage in your Skye Terrier's life, your veterinarian may want to schedule visits twice yearly, instead of once, to run some laboratory screenings, electrocardiograms and the like, and to change the diet to something more digestible. Catching problems early is the best way to manage them effectively. Treating the early stages of heart disease is so much easier than trying to intervene when there is more significant damage to the heart muscle. Similarly, managing the beginning of kidney problems is fairly routine if there is no significant kidney damage. Other problems, like cognitive dysfunction (similar to senility and Alzheimer's disease), cancer, diabetes and arthritis, are more common in older dogs, but all can be treated to help the dog live as many happy, comfortable years as possible. Just as in people, medical management is more effective (and less expensive) when you catch things early.

SELECTING A VETERINARIAN

There is probably no more important decision that you will make regarding your pet's healthcare than the selection of his doctor. Your pet's veterinarian will be a pediatrician, family-practice physician and gerontologist, depending on the dog's life stage, and will be the individual who makes recommendations regarding issues such as when specialists need to be consulted, when diagnostic testing and/or therapeutic intervention is needed and when you will need to seek outside emergency and critical-care services. Your vet will act as your advocate and liaison throughout these processes.

Everyone has his own idea about what to look for in a vet, an individual who will play a big role in his dog's (and, of course, his own) life for many years to come. For some, it is the compassionate caregiver with whom they hope to develop a professional relationship to span the lifetime of their dogs and even their future pets. For others, they are seeking a clinician with keen diagnostic and therapeutic insight who can deliver state-of-the-art healthcare. Still others need a veterinary facility that is open evenings and weekends, is in close proximity or provides mobile veterinary services to accommodate their schedules; these people may not much mind that their dogs might see different veterinarians on each visit. Just as we have different reasons for selecting our own healthcare professionals (e.g., covered by insurance plan, expert in field, convenient location, etc.), we should not expect that there is a one-size-fits-all recommendation for selecting a veterinarian and veterinary practice. The best advice is to be honest in your assessment of what you expect from a veterinary practice and to conscientiously research the options in your area. You will quickly appreciate that not all veterinary practices are the same, and you will be happiest with one that truly meets your needs.

There is another point to be considered in the selection of veterinary services. Not that long ago, a single veterinarian would attempt to manage all medical and

YOUR DOG NEEDS TO VISIT THE VET IF:

- He has ingested a toxin such as antifreeze or a toxic plant; in these cases, administer first aid and call the vet right away
- His teeth are discolored, loose or missing or he has sores or other signs of infection or abnormality in the mouth
- He has been vomiting, has had diarrhea or has been constipated for over 24 hours; call immediately if you notice blood
- He has refused food for over 24 hours
- His eating habits, water intake or toilet habits have noticeably changed; if you have noticed weight gain or weight loss
- He shows symptoms of bloat, which requires *immediate* attention
- He is salivating excessively
- He has a lump in his throat
- He has a lump or bumps anywhere on the body
- He is very lethargic
- He appears to be in pain or otherwise has trouble chewing or swallowing
- His skin loses elasticity

Of course, there will be other instances in which a visit to the vet is necessary; these are just some of the signs that could be indicative of serious problems that need to be caught as early as possible.

surgical issues as they arose. That was often problematic, because veterinarians are trained in many species and many diseases, and it was just impossible for general veterinary practitioners to be experts in every species, every breed, every field and every ailment. However, just as in the human healthcare fields, specialization has allowed general practitioners to concentrate on primary healthcare delivery, especially wellness and the prevention of infectious diseases, and to utilize a network of specialists to assist in the management of conditions that require specific expertise and experience. Thus there are now many types of veterinary specialists, including dermatologists, cardiologists, ophthalmologists, surgeons, internists, oncologists, neurologists, behaviorists, criticalists and others to help primary-care veterinarians deal with complicated medical challenges. In most cases, specialists see cases referred by primary-care veterinarians, make diagnoses and set up management plans. From there, the animals' ongoing care is returned to their primary-care veterinarians. This important team approach to your pet's medical-care needs has provided opportunities for advanced care and an unparalleled level of quality to be delivered.

With all of the opportunities for your Skye Terrier to receive high-quality veterinary medical care, there is another topic that needs to be addressed at the same time—cost. It's been said that you can have excellent healthcare or inexpensive healthcare, but never both; this is as true in veterinary medicine as it is in human medicine. While veterinary costs are a fraction of what the same services cost in the human healthcare arena, it is still difficult to deal with unanticipated medical costs, especially since they can easily creep into hundreds or even thousands of dollars if specialists or emergency services become involved. However, there are ways of managing these risks. The easiest is to buy pet health insurance and realize that its foremost purpose is not to cover routine healthcare visits but rather to serve as an umbrella for those rainy days when your pet needs medical care and you don't want to worry about whether or not you can afford that care.

Pet insurance policies are very cost-effective (and very inexpensive by human health-insurance standards), but make sure that you buy the policy long before you intend to use it (preferably starting in puppyhood, because coverage will exclude pre-existing conditions) and that you are actually buying an indemnity insurance plan from an insurance company that is regulated by your state or province. Many insurance

Common Infectious Diseases

Let's discuss some of the diseases that create the need for vaccination in the first place. Following are the major canine infectious diseases and a simple explanation of each.

Rabies: A devastating viral disease that can be fatal in dogs and people. In fact, vaccination of dogs and cats is an important public-health measure to create a resistant animal buffer population to protect people from contracting the disease. Vaccination schedules are determined on a government level and are not optional for pet owners; rabies vaccination is required by law in all 50 states.

Parvovirus: A severe, potentially life-threatening disease that is easily transmitted between dogs. There are four strains of the virus, but it is believed that there is significant "cross-protection" between strains that may be included in individual vaccines.

Distemper: A potentially severe and life-threatening disease with a relatively high risk of exposure, especially in certain regions. In very high-risk distemper environments, young pups may be vaccinated with human measles vaccine, a related virus that offers cross-protection when administered at four to ten weeks of age.

Hepatitis: Caused by canine adenovirus type 1 (CAV-1), but since vaccination with the causative virus has a higher rate of adverse effects, cross-protection is derived from the use of adenovirus type 2 (CAV-2), a cause of respiratory disease and one of the potential causes of canine cough. Vaccination with CAV-2 provides long-term immunity against hepatitis, but relatively less protection against respiratory infection.

Canine cough: Also called tracheobronchitis, actually a fairly complicated result of viral and bacterial offenders; therefore, even with vaccination, protection is incomplete. Wherever dogs congregate, canine cough will likely be spread among them. Intranasal vaccination with *Bordetella* and parainfluenza is the best safeguard, but the duration of immunity does not appear to be very long, typically a year at most. These are non-core vaccines, but vaccination is sometimes mandated by boarding kennels, obedience classes, dog shows and other places where dogs congregate to try to minimize spread of infection.

Leptospirosis: A potentially fatal disease that is more common in some geographic regions. It is capable of being spread to humans. The disease varies with the individual "serovar," or strain, of *Leptospira* involved. Since there does not appear to be much cross-protection between serovars, protection is only as good as the likelihood that the serovar in the vaccine is the same as the one in the pet's local environment. Problems with *Leptospira* vaccines are that protection does not last very long, side effects are not uncommon and a large percentage of dogs (perhaps 30%) may not respond to vaccination.

Borrelia burgdorferi: The cause of Lyme disease, the risk of which varies with the geographic area in which the pet lives and travels. Lyme disease is spread by deer ticks in the eastern US and western black-legged ticks in the western part of the country, and the risk of exposure is high in some regions. Lameness, fever and inappetence are most commonly seen in affected dogs. The extent of protection from the vaccine has not been conclusively demonstrated.

Coronavirus: This disease has a high risk of exposure, especially in areas where dogs congregate, but it typically causes only mild to moderate digestive upset (diarrhea, vomiting, etc.). Vaccines are available, but the duration of protection is believed to be relatively short and the effectiveness of the vaccine in preventing infection is considered low.

There are many other vaccinations available, including those for *Giardia* and canine adenovirus-1. While there may be some specific indications for their use, and local risk factors to be considered, they are not widely recommended for most dogs.

policy look-alikes are actually discount clubs that are redeemable only at specific locations and for specific services. An indemnity plan covers your pet at almost all veterinary, specialty and emergency practices and is an excellent way to manage your pet's ongoing healthcare needs.

VACCINATIONS AND INFECTIOUS DISEASES

There has never been an easier time to prevent a variety of infectious diseases in your dog, but the advances we've made in veterinary medicine come with a price—choice. Now while it may seem that choice is a good thing (and it is), it has never been more difficult for the pet owner (or the veterinarian) to make an informed decision about the best way to protect pets through vaccination.

Years ago, it was just accepted that puppies got a starter series of vaccinations and then annual "boosters" throughout their lives to keep them protected. As more and more vaccines became available, consumers wanted the convenience of having all of that protection in a single injection. The result was "multivalent" vaccines that crammed a lot of protection into a single syringe. The manufacturers' recommendations were to give the vaccines annually, and this was a simple enough protocol to follow. However, as veterinary medicine has become more sophisticated and we have started looking more at healthcare quandaries rather than convenience, it became necessary to reevaluate the situation and deal with some tough questions. It is important to realize that whether or not to use a particular vaccine depends on the risk of contracting the disease against which it protects, the severity of the disease if it is contracted, the duration of immunity provided by the vaccine, the safety of the product and the needs of the individual animal. In a very general sense, rabies, distemper, hepatitis and parvovirus are considered core vaccine needs, while parainfluenza, *Bordetella bronchiseptica*, leptospirosis, coronavirus and borreliosis (Lyme disease) are considered non-core needs and best reserved for animals that demonstrate reasonable risk of contracting the diseases.

NEUTERING/SPAYING

Sterilization procedures (neutering for males/spaying for females) are meant to accomplish several purposes. While the underlying premise is to address the risk of pet overpopulation, there are also some medical and behavioral benefits to the surgeries as well. For females, spaying prior to the first estrus (heat cycle) leads to a marked reduction in the risk of mammary cancer and other serious female health problems. There also will be no manifestations of "heat" to attract male dogs and no bleeding in the house. For males, there is prevention of testicular cancer and a reduction in the risk of prostate problems. In both sexes there may be some limited reduction in aggressive behaviors toward other dogs, and some diminishing of urine marking, roaming and mounting.

While neutering and spaying do indeed prevent animals from contributing to pet overpopulation, even no-cost and low-cost neutering options have not eliminated the problem. Perhaps one of the main reasons for this is that individuals that intentionally breed their dogs and those that allow their animals to run at large are the main causes of unwanted offspring. Also, animals in shelters are often there because they were abandoned or relinquished, not because they came from unplanned matings. Neutering/spaying is important, but it should be considered in the context of the real causes of animals' ending up in shelters and eventually being euthanized.

One of the important considerations regarding neutering is that it is a surgical procedure. This sometimes gets lost in discussions of low-cost procedures and commoditization of the process. In females, spaying is specifically referred to as an ovariohysterectomy. In this procedure, a midline incision is made in the abdomen and the entire uterus and both ovaries are surgically removed. While this is a major invasive surgical procedure, it usually has few complications, because it is typically performed on healthy young animals. However, it is major surgery, as any woman who has had a hysterectomy will attest.

In males, neutering has traditionally referred to castration, which involves the surgical removal of both testicles. While still a significant piece of surgery, there is not the abdominal exposure that is required in the female surgery. In addition, there is now a chemical sterilization option, in which a solution is injected into each testicle, leading to atrophy of the sperm-producing cells. This can typically be done under sedation rather than full anesthesia. This is a relatively new approach, and there are no long-term clinical studies yet available.

Neutering/spaying is typically done around six months of age at most veterinary hospitals, although techniques have been pioneered to perform the procedures in animals as young as eight weeks of age. In general, the surgeries on the very young animals are done for the specific reason of sterilizing them before they go to their new homes. This is done in some shelter hospitals for assurance that the animals will definitely not produce any pups. Otherwise, these organizations need to rely on owners to comply with their wishes to have the animals "altered" at a later date, something that does not always happen.

There are some exciting immunocontraceptive "vaccines" currently under development, and there may be a time when contraception in pets will not require surgical procedures. We anxiously await these developments.

If your Skye Terrier is shaking his head, he may be trying to tell you something. Perhaps it's ear mites, an uncommon itch or a new dance craze!

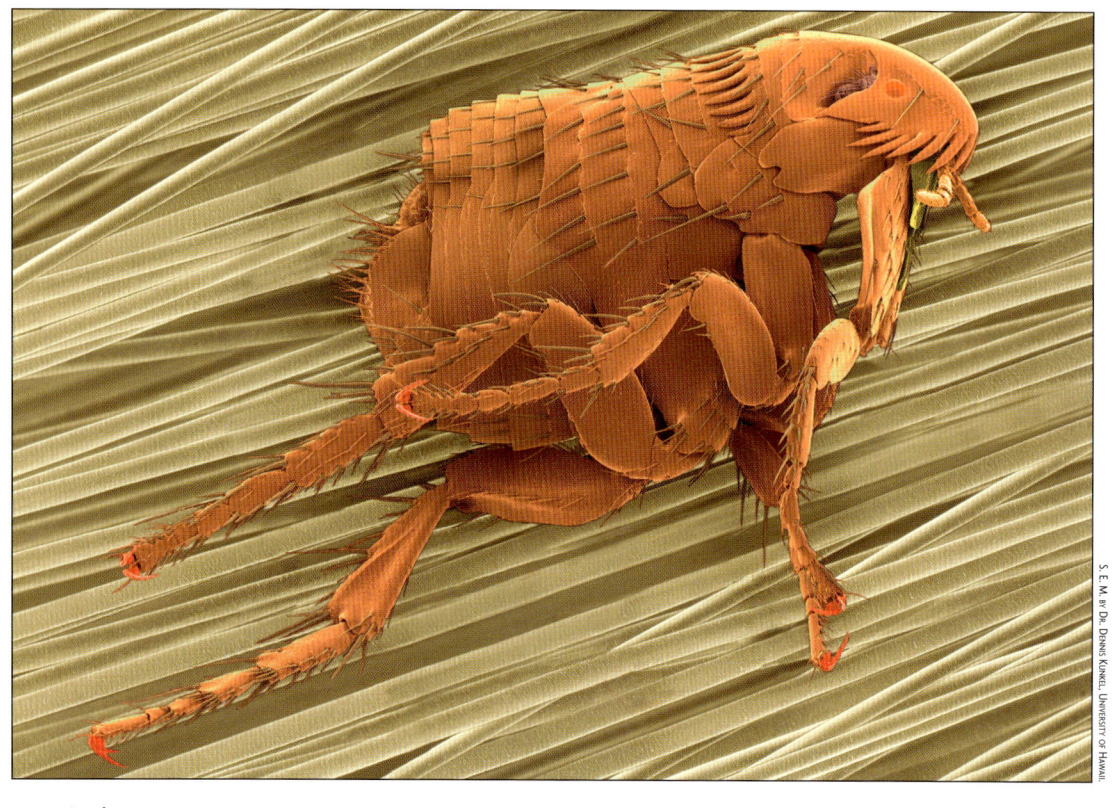

A scanning electron micrograph of a dog flea, *Ctenocephalides canis*, on dog hair.

EXTERNAL PARASITES

FLEAS

Fleas have been around for millions of years and, while we have better tools now for controlling them than at any time in the past, there still is little chance that they will end up on an endangered species list. Actually, they are very well adapted to living on our pets, and they continue to adapt as we make advances.

The female flea can consume 15 times her weight in blood during active reproduction and can lay as many as 40 eggs a day. These eggs are very resistant to the effects of insecticides. They hatch into larvae, which then mature and spin cocoons. The immature fleas reside in this pupal stage until the time is right for feeding. This pupal stage is also very resistant to the effects of insecticides, and pupae can last in the environment without feeding for many months. Newly emergent fleas are attracted to animals by the warmth of the animals' bodies, movement and exhaled carbon dioxide. However, when they first emerge from their cocoons, they orient towards light; thus when an animal passes between a flea and the light source, casting a shadow, the flea pounces and starts to feed. If the animal turns out to be a dog or cat, the reproductive cycle continues. If the flea lands on another type of animal, including a person, the flea will bite but will then look for a more appropriate host. An emerging adult flea can survive without feeding for up to 12 months but, once it tastes blood, it can survive off its host for only 3 to 4 days.

It was once thought that fleas spend most of their lives in the environment, but we now know that fleas won't willingly jump off a dog unless leaping to another dog or when physically removed by brushing, bathing or other manipulation. Flea eggs, on the other hand, are shiny and smooth, and they roll off the animal and into the environment. The eggs, larvae and pupae then exist in the environment, but once the adult finds a susceptible animal, it's home sweet home until the flea is forced to seek refuge elsewhere.

Since adult fleas live on the animal and immature forms survive in the environment, a successful treatment plan must address all stages of the flea life cycle. There are now several safe and effective flea-control products that can be applied on a monthly basis. These include fipronil, imidacloprid, selamectin and permethrin (found in several formulations). Most of these products have significant flea-killing rates within 24 hours. However, none of them will control the immature forms in the environment. To accomplish this, there are a variety of insect growth regulators that can be sprayed into

> **FLEA PREVENTION FOR YOUR DOG**
> - Discuss with your veterinarian the safest product to protect your dog, likely in the form of a monthly tablet or a liquid preparation placed on the back of the dog's neck.
> - For dogs suffering from flea-bite dermatitis, a shampoo or topical insecticide treatment is required.
> - Your lawn and property should be sprayed with an insecticide designed to kill fleas and ticks that lurk outdoors.
> - Using a flea comb, check the dog's coat regularly for any signs of parasites.
> - Practice good housekeeping. Vacuum floors, carpets and furniture regularly, especially in the areas that the dog frequents, and wash the dog's bedding weekly.
> - Follow up house-cleaning with carpet shampoos and sprays to rid the house of fleas at all stages of development. Insect growth regulators are the safest option.

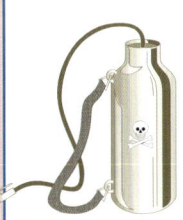

THE FLEA'S LIFE CYCLE

What came first, the flea or the egg? This age-old mystery is more difficult to comprehend than the actual cycle of the flea. Fleas usually live only about four months. A female can lay 2,000 eggs in her lifetime.

Egg

After ten days of rolling around your carpet or under your furniture, the eggs hatch into larvae, which feed on various and sundry debris. In days or months, depending on the climate, the larvae spin cocoons and develop into the pupal or nymph stage, which quickly develop into fleas.

Larva

Pupa

These immature fleas must locate a host within 10 to 14 days or they will die. Only about 1% of the flea population exist as adult fleas, while the other 99% exist as eggs, larvae or pupae.

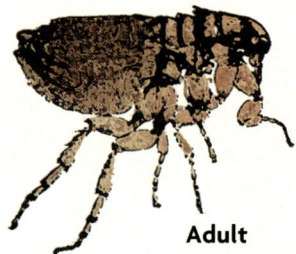
Adult

KILL FLEAS THE NATURAL WAY

If you choose not to go the route of conventional medication, there are some natural ways to ward off fleas:
- Dust your dog with a natural flea powder, composed of such herbal goodies as rosemary, wormwood, pennyroyal, citronella, rue, tobacco powder and eucalyptus.
- Apply diatomaceous earth, the fossilized remains of single-cell algae, to your carpets, furniture and pet's bedding. Even though it's not good for dogs, it's even worse for fleas, which will dry up swiftly and die.
- Brush your dog frequently, give him adequate exercise and let him fast occasionally. All of these activities strengthen the dog's immune system and make him more resistant to disease and parasites.
- Bathe your dog with a capful of pennyroyal or eucalyptus oil.
- Feed a natural diet, free of additives and preservatives. Add some fresh garlic and brewer's yeast to the dog's morning portion, as these items have flea-repelling properties.

the environment (e.g., pyriproxyfen, methoprene, fenoxycarb) as well as insect development inhibitors such as lufenuron that can be administered. These compounds have no effect on adult fleas, but they stop immature forms from developing into adults. In years gone by, we relied heavily on toxic insecticides (such as organophosphates, organochlorines and carbamates) to manage the flea problem, but today's options are not only much safer to use on our pets but also safer for the environment.

Healthcare

TICKS

Ticks are members of the spider class (arachnids) and are blood-sucking parasites capable of transmitting a variety of diseases, including Lyme disease, ehrlichiosis, babesiosis and Rocky Mountain spotted fever. It's easy to see ticks on your own skin, but it is more of a challenge when your furry companion is affected. Whenever you happen to be planning a stroll in a tick-infested area (especially forests, grassy or wooded areas or parks) be prepared to do a thorough inspection of your dog afterward to search for ticks. Ticks can be tricky, so make sure you spend time looking in the ears, between the toes and everywhere else where a tick might hide. Ticks need to be attached for 24–72 hours before they transmit most of the diseases that they carry, so you do have a window of opportunity for some preventive intervention.

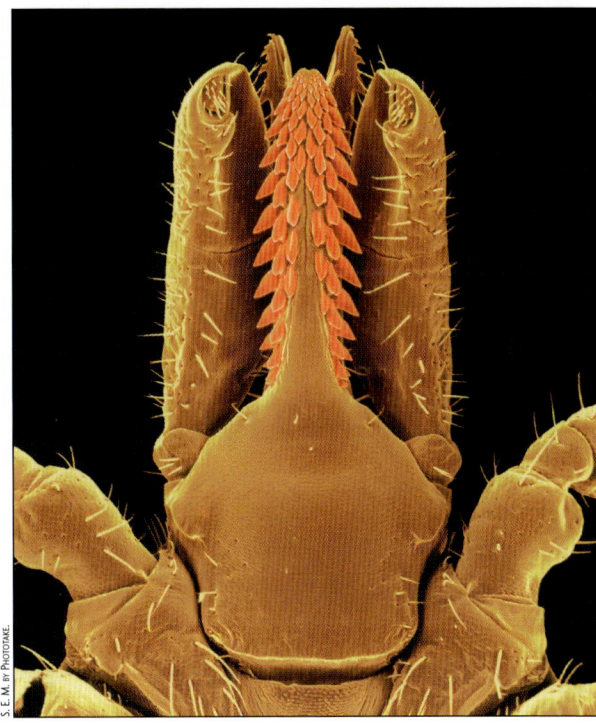

A scanning electron micrograph of the head of a female deer tick, *Ixodes dammini*, a parasitic tick that carries Lyme disease.

A TICKING BOMB

There is nothing good about a tick's harpooning his nose into your dog's skin. Among the diseases caused by ticks are Rocky Mountain spotted fever, canine ehrlichiosis, canine babesiosis, canine hepatozoonosis and Lyme disease. If a dog is allergic to the saliva of a female wood tick, he can develop tick paralysis.

Female ticks live to eat and breed. They can lay between 4,000 and 5,000 eggs and they die soon after. Males, on the other hand, live only to mate with the females and continue the process as long as they are able. Most ticks live on multiple hosts before parasitizing dogs. The immature forms typically reside on grass and shrubs, waiting for susceptible animals to walk by. The larvae and nymph stages typically feed on wildlife.

If only a few ticks are present on a dog, they can be plucked out, but it is important to remove the entire head and mouthparts,

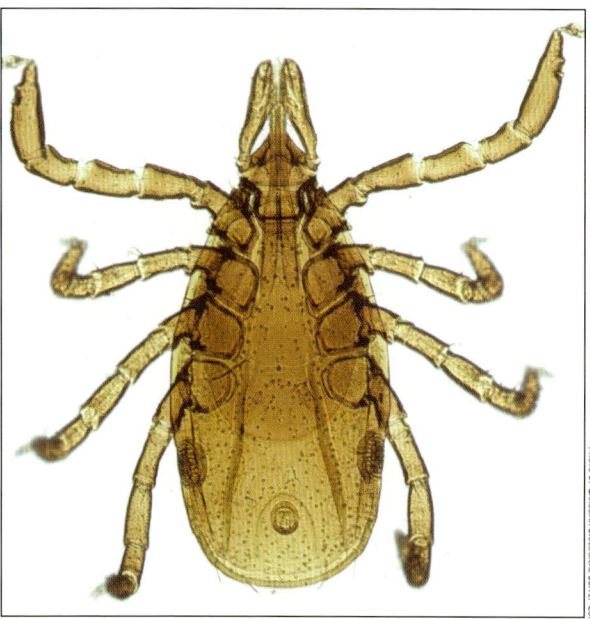

Deer tick, Ixodes dammini.

which may be deeply embedded in the skin. This is best accomplished with forceps designed especially for this purpose; fingers can be used but should be protected with rubber gloves, plastic wrap or at least a paper towel. The tick should be grasped as closely as possible to the animal's skin and should be pulled upward with steady, even pressure. Do not squeeze, crush or puncture the body of the tick or you risk exposure to any disease carried by that tick. Once the ticks have been removed, the sites of attachment should be disinfected. Your hands should then be washed with soap and water to further minimize risk of contagion. The tick should be disposed of in a container of alcohol or household bleach.

Some of the newer flea products, specifically those with fipronil, selamectin and permethrin, have effect against some, but not all, species of tick. Flea collars containing appropriate pesticides (e.g., propoxur, chlorfenvinphos) can aid in tick control. In most areas, such collars should be placed on animals in March, at the beginning of the tick season, and changed regularly. Leaving the collar on when the pesticide level is waning invites the development of resistance. Amitraz collars are also good for tick control, and the active ingredient does not interfere with other flea-control products. The ingredient helps prevent the attachment of ticks to the skin and will cause those ticks already on the skin to detach themselves.

TICK CONTROL
Removal of underbrush and leaf litter and the thinning of trees in areas where tick control is desired are recommended. These actions remove the cover and food sources for small animals that serve as hosts for ticks. With continued mowing of grasses in these areas, the probability of ticks' surviving is further reduced. A variety of insecticide ingredients (e.g., resmethrin, carbaryl, permethrin, chlorpyrifos, dioxathion and allethrin) are registered for tick control around the home.

MITES

Mites are tiny arachnid parasites that parasitize the skin of dogs. Skin diseases caused by mites are referred to as "mange," and there are many different forms seen in dogs. These forms are very different from one another, each one warranting an individual description.

Sarcoptic mange, or scabies, is one of the itchiest conditions that affects dogs. The microscopic *Sarcoptes* mites burrow into the superficial layers of the skin and can drive dogs crazy with itchiness. They are also communicable to people, although they can't complete their reproductive cycle on people. In addition to being tiny, the mites also are often difficult to find when trying to make a diagnosis. Skin scrapings from multiple areas are examined microscopically but, even then, sometimes the mites cannot be found.

Fortunately, scabies is relatively easy to treat, and there are a variety of products that will successfully kill the mites. Since the mites can't live in the environment for very long without feeding, a complete cure is usually possible within four to eight weeks.

Cheyletiellosis is caused by a relatively large mite, which sometimes can be seen even without a microscope. Often referred to as "walking dandruff," this also causes itching, but not usually as profound as with scabies. While *Cheyletiella*

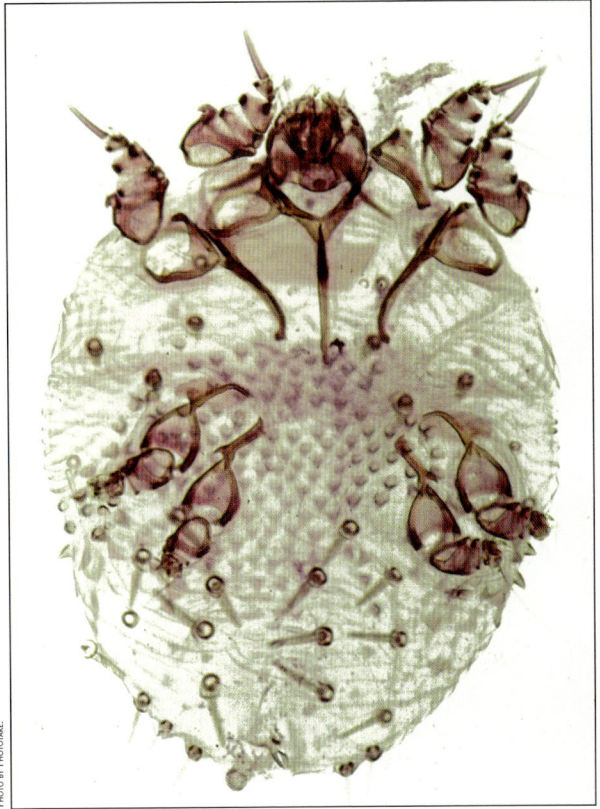

Sarcoptes scabiei, commonly known as the "itch mite."

mites can survive somewhat longer in the environment than scabies mites, they too are relatively easy to treat, being responsive to not only the medications used to treat scabies but also often to flea-control products.

Otodectes cynotis is the canine ear mite and is one of the more common causes of mange, especially in young dogs in shelters or pet stores. That's because the mites are typically present in large numbers and are quickly spread to nearby animals. The mites rarely do

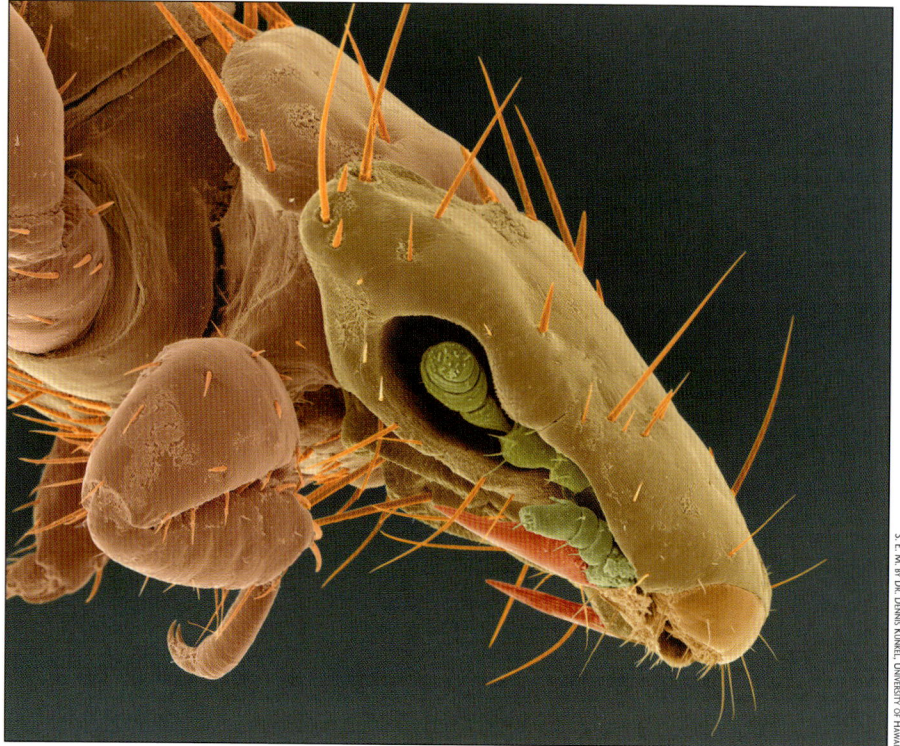

Micrograph of a dog louse, *Heterodoxus spiniger*. Female lice attach their eggs to the hairs of the dog. As the eggs hatch, the larval lice bite and feed on the blood. Lice can also feed on dead skin and hair. This feeding activity can cause hair loss and skin problems.

much harm but can be difficult to eradicate if the treatment regimen is not comprehensive. While many try to treat the condition with ear drops only, this is the most common cause of treatment failure. Ear drops cause the mites to simply move out of the ears and as far away as possible (usually to the base of the tail) until the insecticide levels in the ears drop to an acceptable level—then it's back to business as usual! The successful treatment of ear mites requires treating all animals in the household with a systemic insecticide, such as selamectin, or a combination of miticidal ear drops combined with whole-body flea-control preparations.

Demodicosis, sometimes referred to as red mange, can be one of the most difficult forms of mange to treat. Part of the problem has to do with the fact that the mites live in the hair follicles and they are relatively well shielded from topical and systemic products. The main issue, however, is that demodectic mange typically results only when there is some underlying process interfering with the dog's immune system.

Since *Demodex* mites are normal residents of the skin of

mammals, including humans, there is usually a mite population explosion only when the immune system fails to keep the number of mites in check. In young animals, the immune deficit may be transient or may reflect an actual inherited immune problem. In older animals, demodicosis is usually seen only when there is another disease hampering the immune system, such as diabetes, cancer, thyroid problems or the use of immune-suppressing drugs. Accordingly, treatment involves not only trying to kill the mange mites but also discerning what is interfering with immune function and correcting it if possible.

Chiggers represent several different species of mite that don't parasitize dogs specifically, but do latch on to passersby and can cause irritation. The problem is most prevalent in wooded areas in the late summer and fall. Treatment is not difficult, as the mites do not complete their life cycle on dogs and are susceptible to a variety of miticidal products.

MOSQUITOES

Mosquitoes have long been known to transmit a variety of diseases to people, as well as just being biting pests during warm weather. They also pose a real risk to pets. Not only do they carry deadly heartworms but recently there also has been much concern over their involvement with West Nile virus. While we can avoid heartworm with the use of preventive medications, there are no such preventives for West Nile virus. The only method of prevention in endemic areas is active mosquito control. Fortunately, most dogs that have been exposed to the virus only developed flu-like symptoms and, to date, there have not been the large number of reported deaths in canines as seen in some other species.

Illustration of *Demodex folliculoram.*

MOSQUITO REPELLENT

Low concentrations of DEET (less than 10%), found in many human mosquito repellents, have been safely used on dogs but, in these concentrations, probably give only about two hours of protection. DEET may be safe in these small concentrations, but since it is not licensed for use on dogs, there is no research proving its safety for dogs. Products containing permethrin give the longest-lasting protection, perhaps two to four weeks. As DEET is not licensed for use on dogs, and both DEET and permethrin can be quite toxic to cats, appropriate care should be exercised. Other products, such as those containing oil of citronella, also have some mosquito-repellent activity, but typically have a relatively short duration of action.

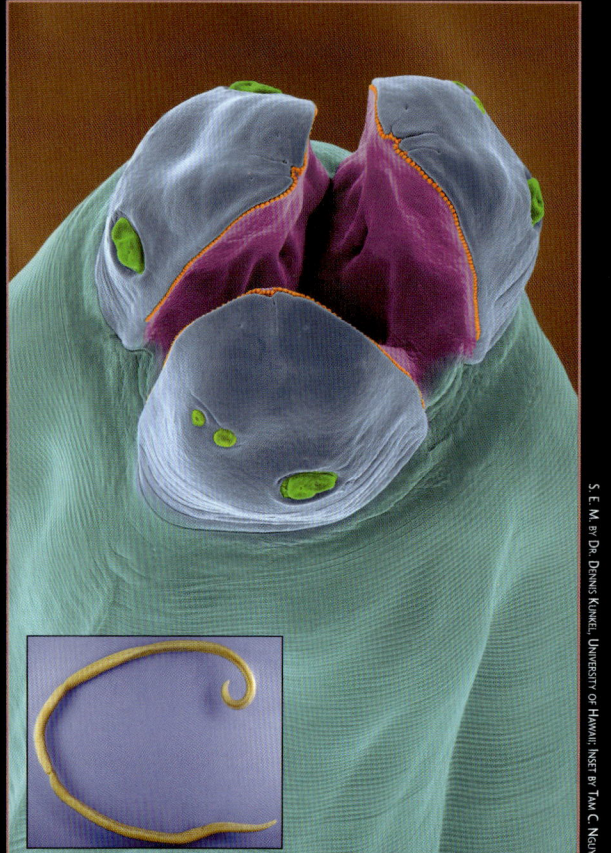

The ascarid roundworm Toxocara canis, showing the mouth with three lips. INSET: Photomicrograph of the roundworm Ascaris lumbricoides.

ASCARID DANGERS

The most commonly encountered worms in dogs are roundworms known as ascarids. *Toxascaris leonine* and *Toxocara canis* are the two species that infect dogs. Subsisting in the dog's stomach and intestines, adult roundworms can grow to 7 inches in length and adult females can lay in excess of 200,000 eggs in a single day.

In humans, visceral larval migrans affects people who have ingested eggs of *Toxocara canis*, which frequently contaminates children's sandboxes, beaches and park grounds. The roundworms reside in the human's stomach and intestines, as they would in a dog's, but do not mature. Instead, they find their way to the liver, lungs and skin, or even to the heart or kidneys in severe cases. Deworming puppies is critical in preventing the infection in humans, and young children should never handle nursing pups who have not been dewormed.

INTERNAL PARASITES: WORMS

ASCARIDS

Ascarids are intestinal roundworms that rarely cause severe disease in dogs. Nonetheless, they are of major public health significance because they can be transferred to people. Sadly, it is children who are most commonly affected by the parasite, probably from inadvertently ingesting ascarid-contaminated soil. In fact, many yards and children's sandboxes contain appreciable numbers of ascarid eggs. So, while ascarids don't bite dogs or latch onto their intestines to suck blood, they do cause some nasty medical conditions in children and are best eradicated from our furry friends. Because pups can start passing ascarid eggs by three weeks of age, most parasite-control programs begin at two weeks of age and are repeated every two weeks until pups are eight weeks old. It is important to

HOOKED ON ANCYLOSTOMA

Adult dogs can become infected by the bloodsucking nematodes we commonly call hookworms via ingesting larvae from the ground or via the larvae penetrating the dog's skin. It is not uncommon for infected dogs to show no symptoms of hookworm infestation. Sometimes symptoms occur within ten days of exposure. These symptoms can include bloody diarrhea, anemia, loss of weight and general weakness. Dogs pass the hookworm eggs in their stools, which serves as the vet's method of identifying the infestation. The hookworm larvae can encyst themselves in the dog's tissues and be released when the dog is experiencing stress.

Caused by an *Ancylostoma* species whose common host is the dog, cutaneous larval migrans affects humans, causing itching and lumps and streaks beneath the surface of the skin.

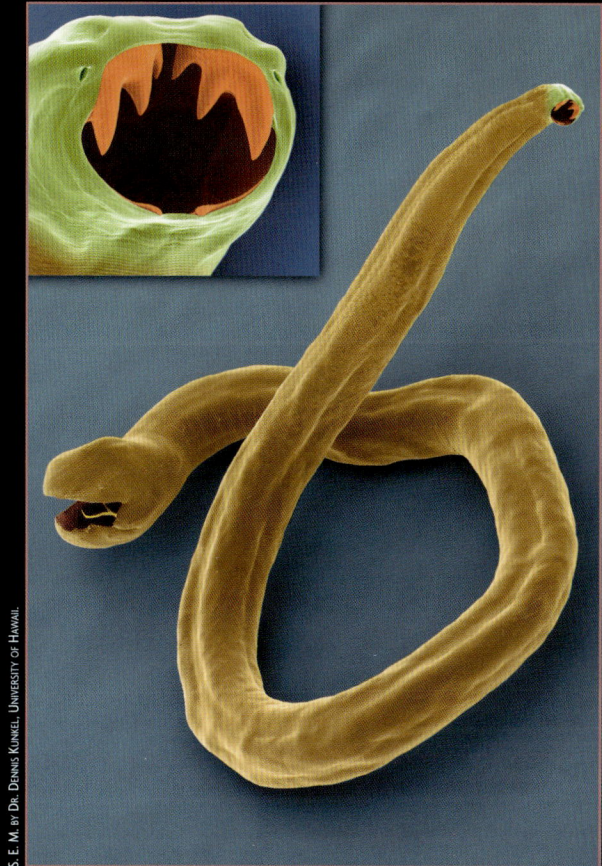

The hookworm *Ancylostoma caninum* infests the intestines of dogs. INSET: Note the row of hooks at the posterior end, used to anchor the worm to the intestinal wall.

realize that bitches can pass ascarids to their pups even if they test negative prior to whelping. Accordingly, bitches are best treated at the same time as the pups.

HOOKWORMS

Unlike ascarids, hookworms do latch onto a dog's intestinal tract and can cause significant loss of blood and protein. Similar to ascarids, hookworms can be transmitted to humans, where they cause a condition known as cutaneous larval migrans. Dogs can become infected either by consuming the infective larvae or by the larvae's penetrating the skin directly. People most often get infected when they are lying on the ground (such as on a beach) and the larvae penetrate the skin. Yes, the larvae can penetrate through a beach blanket. Hookworms are typically susceptible to the same medications used to treat ascarids.

WHIPWORMS

Whipworms latch onto the lower aspects of the dog's colon and can cause cramping and diarrhea. Eggs do not start to appear in the dog's feces until about three months after the dog was infected. This worm has a peculiar life cycle, which makes it more difficult to control than ascarids or hookworms. The good thing is that whipworms rarely are transferred to people.

Some of the medications used to treat ascarids and hookworms are also effective against whipworms, but, in general, a separate treatment protocol is needed. Since most of the medications are effective against the adults but not the eggs or larvae, treatment is typically repeated in three weeks, and then often in three months as well. Unfortunately, since dogs don't develop resistance to whipworms, it is difficult to prevent them from getting reinfected if they visit soil contaminated with whipworm eggs.

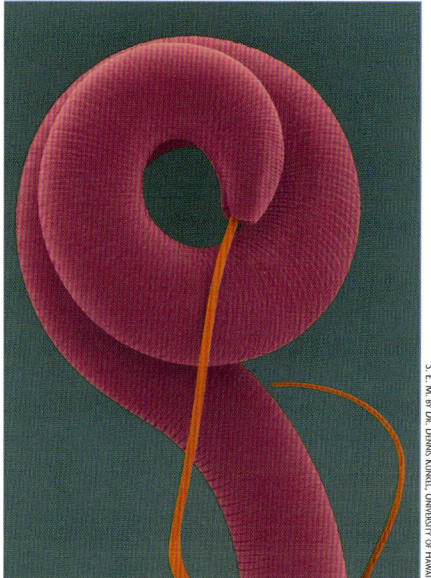

Adult whipworm, *Trichuris* sp., an intestinal parasite.

WORM-CONTROL GUIDELINES
- Practice sanitary habits with your dog and home.
- Clean up after your dog and don't let him sniff or eat other dogs' droppings.
- Control insects and fleas in the dog's environment. Fleas, lice, cockroaches, beetles, mice and rats can act as hosts for various worms.
- Prevent dogs from eating uncooked meat, raw poultry and dead animals.
- Keep dogs and children from playing in sand and soil.
- Kennel dogs on cement or gravel; avoid dirt runs.
- Administer heartworm preventives regularly.
- Have your vet examine your dog's stools at your annual visits.
- Select a boarding kennel carefully so as to avoid contamination from other dogs or an unsanitary environment.
- Prevent dogs from roaming. Obey local leash laws.

TAPEWORMS

There are many different species of tapeworm that affect dogs, but *Dipylidium caninum* is probably the most common and is spread by fleas. Flea larvae feed on organic debris and tapeworm eggs in the environment and, when a dog chews at himself and manages to ingest fleas, he might get a dose of tapeworm at the same time. The tapeworm then develops further in the intestine of the dog.

The tapeworm itself, which is a parasitic flatworm that latches onto the intestinal wall, is composed of numerous segments. When the segments break off into the intestine (as proglottids), they may accumulate around the rectum, like grains of rice. While this tapeworm is disgusting in its behavior, it is not directly communicable to humans (although humans can also get infected by swallowing fleas).

A much more dangerous flatworm is *Echinococcus multilocularis*, which is typically found in foxes, coyotes and wolves. The eggs are passed in the feces and infect rodents, and, when dogs eat the rodents, the dogs can be infected by thousands of adult tapeworms. While the parasites don't cause many problems in dogs, this is considered the most lethal worm infection that people can get. Take appropriate precautions if you live in an area in which these tapeworms are found. Do not use mulch that may contain feces of dogs, cats or wildlife, and discourage your pets from hunting wildlife. Treat these tapeworm infections aggressively in pets, because if humans get infected, approximately half die.

Heartworms

Heartworm disease is caused by the parasite *Dirofilaria immitis* and is seen in dogs around the world. A member of the roundworm group, it is spread between dogs by the bite of an infected mosquito. The mosquito injects infective larvae into the dog's skin with its bite, and these larvae develop under the skin for a period of time before making their way to the heart. There they develop into adults, which grow and create blockages of the heart, lungs and major blood vessels there. They also start producing offspring (microfilariae),

A dog tapeworm proglottid (body segment).

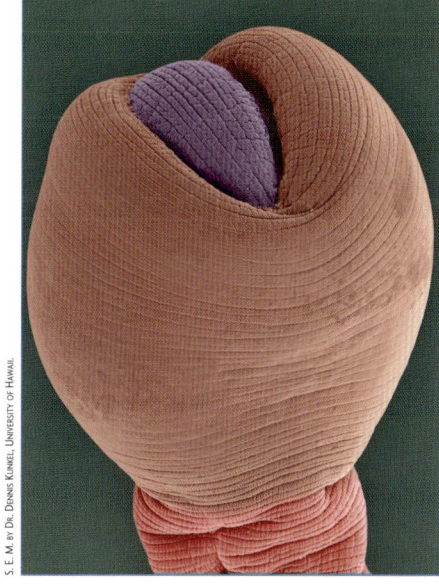

The dog tapeworm *Taenia pisiformis*.

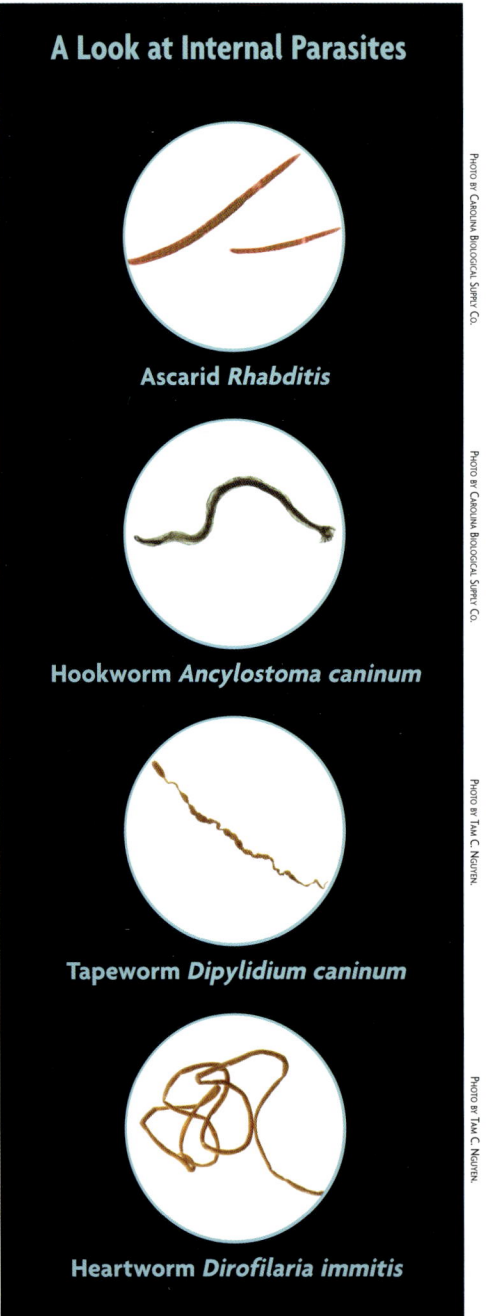

A Look at Internal Parasites

Ascarid *Rhabditis*

Hookworm *Ancylostoma caninum*

Tapeworm *Dipylidium caninum*

Heartworm *Dirofilaria immitis*

PHOTO BY CAROLINA BIOLOGICAL SUPPLY CO.
PHOTO BY CAROLINA BIOLOGICAL SUPPLY CO.
PHOTO BY TAM C. NGUYEN
PHOTO BY TAM C. NGUYEN

and these microfilariae circulate in the bloodstream, waiting to hitch a ride when the next mosquito bites. Once in the mosquito, the microfilariae develop into infective larvae and the entire process is repeated.

When dogs get infected with heartworm, over time they tend to develop symptoms associated with heart disease, such as coughing, exercise intolerance and potentially many other manifestations. Diagnosis is confirmed by either seeing the microfilariae themselves in blood samples or using immunologic tests (antigen testing) to identify the presence of adult heartworms. Since antigen tests measure the presence of adult heartworms and microfilarial tests measure offspring produced by adults, neither are positive until six to seven months after the initial infection. However, the beginning of damage can occur by fifth-stage larvae as early as three months after infection. Thus it is possible for dogs to be harboring problem-causing larvae for up to three months before either type of test would identify an infection.

The good news is that there are great protocols available for preventing heartworm in dogs. Testing is critical in the process, and it is important to understand the benefits as well as the limitations of such testing. All dogs six months of age or older that have not been on continuous heartworm-preventive medication should be

Healthcare

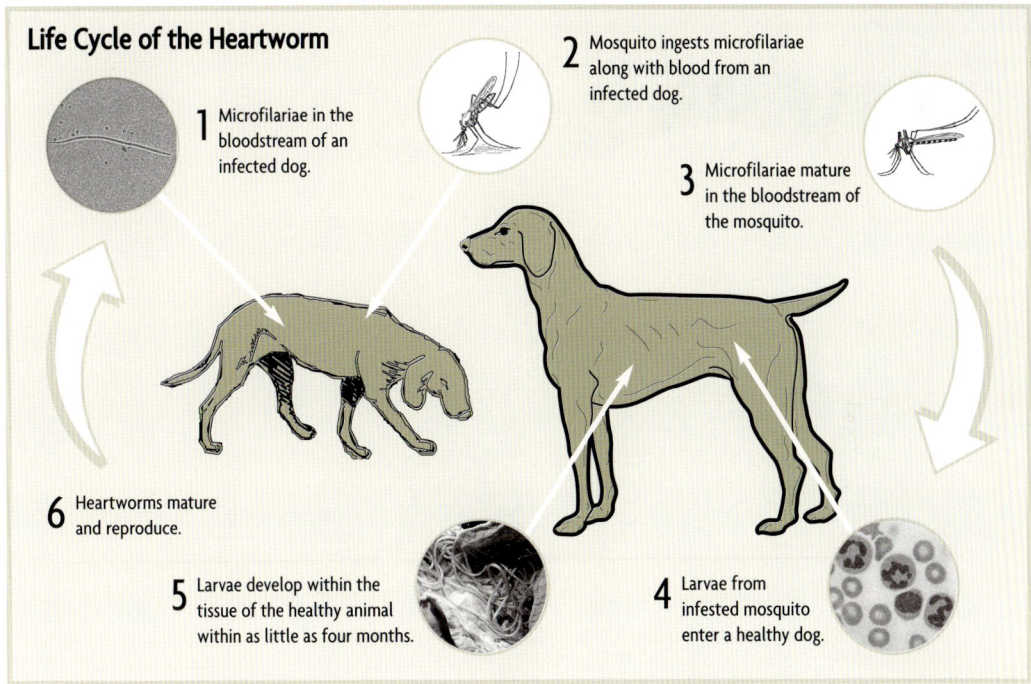

screened with microfilarial or antigen tests. For dogs receiving preventive medication, periodic antigen testing helps assess the effectiveness of the preventives. The American Heartworm Society guidelines suggest that annual retesting may not be necessary when owners have absolutely provided continuous heartworm prevention. Retesting on a two- to three-year interval may be sufficient in these cases. However, your veterinarian will likely have specific guidelines under which heartworm preventives will be prescribed, and many prefer to err on the side of safety and retest annually.

It is indeed fortunate that heartworm is relatively easy to prevent, because treatments can be as life-threatening as the disease itself. Treatment requires a two-step process that kills the adult heartworms first and then the microfilariae. Prevention is obviously preferable; this involves a once-monthly oral or topical treatment. The most common oral preventives include ivermectin (not suitable for some breeds), moxidectin and milbemycin oxime; the once-a-month topical drug selamectin provides heartworm protection in addition to flea, some types of tick and other parasite controls.

THE ABCs OF Emergency Care

Abrasions
Clean wound with running water or 3% hydrogen peroxide. Pat dry with gauze and spray with antibiotic. Do not cover.

Animal Bites
Clean area with soap and saline solution or water. Apply pressure to any bleeding area. Apply antibiotic ointment. Identify biting animal and contact the vet.

Antifreeze Poisoning
Induce vomiting and take dog to the vet.

Bee Sting
Remove stinger and apply soothing lotion or cold compress; give antihistamine in proper dosage.

Bleeding
Apply pressure directly to wound with gauze or towel for five to ten minutes. If wound does not stop bleeding, wrap wound with gauze and adhesive tape.

Bloat/Gastric Torsion
Immediately take the dog to the vet or emergency clinic; phone from car. No time to waste.

Burns
Chemical: Bathe dog with water and pet shampoo. Rinse in saline solution. Apply antibiotic ointment.

Acid: Rinse with water. Apply one part baking soda, two parts water to affected area.

Alkali: Rinse with water. Apply one part vinegar, four parts water to affected area.

Electrical: Apply antibiotic ointment. Seek veterinary assistance immediately.

Choking
If the dog is on the verge of collapsing, wedge a solid object, such as the handle of a screwdriver, between molars on one side of mouth to keep mouth open. Pull tongue out. Use long-nosed pliers or fingers to remove foreign object. Do not push the object down the dog's throat. For small or medium dogs, hold dog upside down by hind legs and shake firmly to dislodge foreign object.

Chlorine Ingestion
With clean water, rinse the mouth and eyes. Give dog water to drink; contact the vet.

Constipation
Feed dog 2 tablespoons bran flakes with each meal. Encourage drinking water. Mix 1/4-teaspoon mineral oil in dog's food. Contact vet if persists longer than 24 hours.

Diarrhea
Withhold food for 12 to 24 hours. Feed dog anti-diarrheal with eyedropper. When feeding resumes, feed one part boiled hamburger, one part plain cooked rice, 1/4 to 3/4 cup four times daily. Contact vet if persists longer than 24 hours.

Dog Bite
Snip away hair around puncture wound; clean with 3% hydrogen peroxide; apply tincture of iodine. Identify biting dog and call the vet. If wound appears deep, take the dog to the vet.

Frostbite
Wrap the dog in a heavy blanket. Warm affected area with a warm bath for ten minutes. Red color to skin will return with circulation; if tissues are pale after 20 minutes, contact the vet.

Use a portable, durable container large enough to contain all items.

DOG OWNER'S FIRST-AID KIT
- ❏ Gauze bandages/swabs
- ❏ Adhesive and non-adhesive bandages
- ❏ Antibiotic powder
- ❏ Antiseptic wash
- ❏ Hydrogen peroxide 3%
- ❏ Antibiotic ointment
- ❏ Lubricating jelly
- ❏ Rectal thermometer
- ❏ Nylon muzzle
- ❏ Scissors and forceps
- ❏ Eyedropper
- ❏ Syringe
- ❏ Anti-bacterial/fungal solution
- ❏ Saline solution
- ❏ Antihistamine
- ❏ Cotton balls
- ❏ Nail clippers
- ❏ Screwdriver/pen knife
- ❏ Flashlight
- ❏ Emergency phone numbers

Heat Stroke
Submerge the dog (up to his muzzle) in cold water; if no response within ten minutes, contact the vet.

Hot Spots
Mix 2 packets Domeboro® with 2 cups water. Saturate cloth with mixture and apply to hot spots for 15–30 minutes. Apply antibiotic ointment. Repeat every six to eight hours.

Poisonous Plants
Wash affected area with soap and water. Cleanse with alcohol. For foxtail/grass, apply antibiotic ointment. Contact vet if plant was ingested.

Rat Poison Ingestion
Induce vomiting. Keep dog calm, maintain dog's normal body temperature (use blanket or heating pad). Get to the vet for antidote.

Shock
Keep the dog calm and warm; call for veterinary assistance.

Snake Bite
If possible, bandage the area and apply pressure. If the area is not conducive to bandaging, use ice to control bleeding. Get immediate help from the vet.

Tick Removal
Apply flea and tick spray directly on tick. Wait one minute. Using tweezers or wearing plastic gloves, grasp the tick's body firmly and pull out. Apply antibiotic ointment.

Vomiting
Restrict water intake; offer a few ice cubes. Withhold food for next meal. Contact vet if vomiting persists longer than 24 hours.

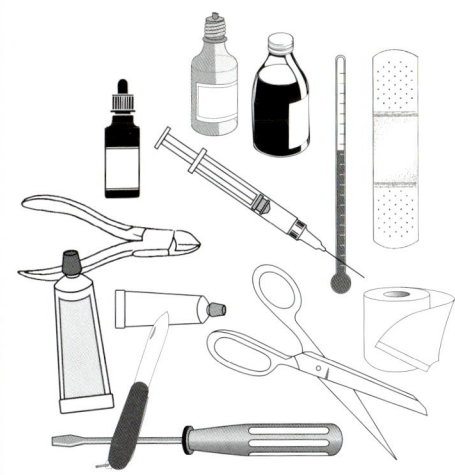

Number-One Killer Disease in Dogs: CANCER

In every age, there is a word associated with a disease or plague that causes humans to shudder. In the 21st century, that word is "cancer." Just as cancer is the leading cause of death in humans, it claims nearly half the lives of dogs that die from a natural disease as well as half the dogs that die over the age of ten years.

Described as a genetic disease, cancer becomes a greater risk as the dog ages. Vets and dog owners have become increasingly aware of the threat of cancer to dogs. Statistics reveal that one dog in every five will develop cancer, the most common of which is skin cancer. Many cancers, including prostate, ovarian and breast cancer, can be avoided by spaying and neutering our dogs by the age of six months.

Early detection of cancer can save or extend a dog's life, so it is absolutely vital for owners to have their dogs examined by a qualified vet or oncologist immediately upon detection of any abnormality. Certain dietary guidelines have also proven to reduce the onset and spread of cancer. Foods based on fish rather than beef, due to the presence of Omega-3 fatty acids, are recommended. Other amino acids such as glutamine have significant benefits for canines, particularly those breeds that show a greater susceptibility to cancer.

Cancer management and treatments promise hope for future generations of canines. Since the disease is genetic, breeders should never breed a dog whose parents, grandparents and any related siblings have developed cancer. It is difficult to know whether to exclude an otherwise healthy dog from a breeding program, as the disease does not manifest itself until the dog's senior years.

RECOGNIZE CANCER WARNING SIGNS

Since early detection can possibly rescue your dog from becoming a cancer statistic, it is essential for owners to recognize the possible signs and seek the assistance of a qualified professional.

- Abnormal bumps or lumps that continue to grow
- Bleeding or discharge from any body cavity
- Persistent stiffness or lameness
- Recurrent sores or sores that do not heal
- Inappetence
- Breathing difficulties
- Weight loss
- Bad breath or odors
- General malaise and fatigue
- Eating and swallowing problems
- Difficulty urinating and defecating

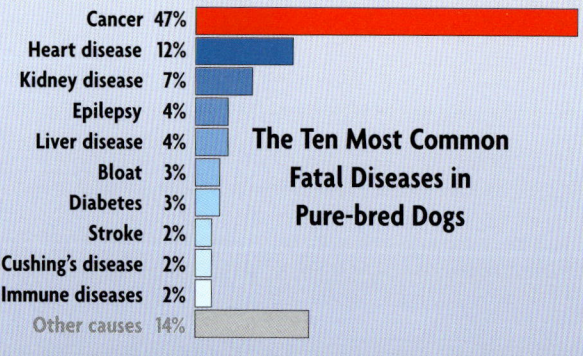

The Ten Most Common Fatal Diseases in Pure-bred Dogs

- Cancer 47%
- Heart disease 12%
- Kidney disease 7%
- Epilepsy 4%
- Liver disease 4%
- Bloat 3%
- Diabetes 3%
- Stroke 2%
- Cushing's disease 2%
- Immune diseases 2%
- Other causes 14%

YOUR SENIOR
SKYE TERRIER

When we bring home a puppy, full of the energy and exuberance that accompanies youth, we hope for a long, happy and fulfilling relationship with the new family member. Even when we adopt an older dog, we look forward to the years of companionship ahead with a new canine friend. However, aging is inevitable for all creatures, and there will come a time when your Skye Terrier reaches his senior years and will need special considerations and attention to his care.

WHEN IS MY DOG A "SENIOR"?
In general, pure-bred dogs are considered to have achieved senior status when they reach 75% of their breed's average lifespan, with lifespan being based on breed size. You can make the generalization that 10 to 12 years is a good lifespan for a Skye, which is not as long as most other terriers. The Skye is rather large for a terrier (despite his lack of leg), and therefore does not enjoy the longevity of his smaller terrier brethren.

Obviously, the old "seven dog years to one human year" theory is not exact. In puppyhood, a dog's year is actually comparable to more than seven human years, considering the puppy's rapid growth during his first year. Then, in adulthood, the ratio decreases. Regardless, the more viable rule of thumb is that the larger the dog, the shorter his expected lifespan. Of course, this can vary among individual dogs, with many living longer than expected, which we hope is the case!

WHAT ARE THE SIGNS OF AGING?
By the time your dog has reached his senior years, you will know him very well, so the physical and behavioral changes that accompany aging should be noticeable to you. Humans and dogs share the most obvious physical sign of aging: gray hair! Graying often occurs first on the muzzle and face, around the eyes. Other telltale signs are the dog's overall decrease in activity. Your older dog might be more content to nap and rest, and he may not show the same old enthusiasm when it's time to play in the yard or go for a walk. Other physical signs include significant weight loss or gain; more labored movement; skin and

coat problems, possibly hair loss; sight and/or hearing problems; changes in toileting habits, perhaps seeming "unhousebroken" at times; and tooth decay, bad breath or other mouth problems.

There are behavioral changes that go along with aging, too. There are numerous causes for behavioral changes. Sometimes a dog's apparent confusion results from a physical change like diminished sight or hearing. If his confusion causes him to be afraid, he may act aggressively or defensively. He may sleep more frequently because his daily walks, though shorter now, tire him out. He may begin to experience separation anxiety or, conversely, become less interested in petting and attention.

There also are clinical conditions that cause behavioral changes in older dogs. One such condition is known as canine cognitive dysfunction (familiarly known as "old-dog" syndrome). It can be frustrating for an owner whose dog is affected with cognitive dysfunction, as it can result in behavioral changes of all types, most seemingly unexplainable. Common changes include the dog's forgetting aspects of the daily routine, such as times to eat, go out for walks, relieve himself and the like. Along the same lines, you may take your dog out at the regular time for a potty trip and he may have no idea why he is there. Sometimes a placid dog will begin to show aggressive or possessive tendencies or, conversely, a hyperactive dog will start to "mellow out."

Disease also can be the cause of behavioral changes in senior dogs. Hormonal problems (Cushing's disease is common in older dogs), diabetes and thyroid disease can cause increased appetite, which can lead to aggression related to food guarding. It's better to be proactive with your senior dog, making more frequent trips to the vet if necessary and having bloodwork done to test for the diseases that can commonly befall older dogs.

This is not to say that, as dogs age, they all fall apart physically and become nasty in personality. The aforementioned changes are discussed to alert owners to the things that may happen as their dogs get older. Many hardy dogs remain active and alert well into old age. However, it can be frustrating and heartbreaking for owners to see their beloved dogs change physically and temperamentally. Just know that it's the same Skye Terrier under there, and that he still loves you and appreciates your care, which he needs now more than ever.

HOW DO I CARE FOR MY AGING DOG?

Again, every dog is an individual in terms of aging. Your dog might

CANINE COGNITIVE DYSFUNCTION

"OLD-DOG SYNDROME"

There are many ways for you to evaluate old-dog syndrome. Veterinarians have defined canine cognitive dysfunction as the gradual deterioration of cognitive abilities, indicated by changes in the dog's behavior. When a dog changes his routine response, and maladies have been eliminated as the cause of these behavioral changes, then canine cognitive dysfunction is the usual diagnosis.

More than half the dogs over eight years old suffer from some form of cognitive dysfunction. The older the dog, the more chance he has of suffering from cognitive dysfunction. In humans, doctors often dismiss the cognitive-dysfunction behavioral changes as part of "winding down."

There are four major signs of canine cognitive dysfunction: frequent potty accidents inside the home, sleeping much more or much less than normal, acting confused and failing to respond to social stimuli. There are medications available to help affected dogs.

SYMPTOMS OF CANINE COGNITIVE DYSFUNCTION

FREQUENT POTTY ACCIDENTS
- Urinates in the house.
- Defecates in the house.
- Doesn't signal that he wants to go out.

FAILURE TO RESPOND TO SOCIAL STIMULI
- Comes to people less frequently, whether called or not.
- Doesn't tolerate petting for more than a short time.
- Doesn't come to the door when you return home.

CONFUSION
- Goes outside and just stands there.
- Appears confused with a faraway look in his eyes.
- Hides more often.
- Doesn't recognize friends.
- Doesn't come when called.
- Walks around listlessly and without a destination.

SLEEP PATTERNS
- Awakens more slowly.
- Sleeps more than normal during the day.
- Sleeps less during the night.

reach the estimated "senior" age for his breed and show no signs of slowing down. However, even if he shows no outward signs of aging, he should begin a senior-care program once he reaches the determined age. He may not show it, but he's not a pup anymore! By providing him with extra attention to his veterinary care at this age, you will be practicing good preventive medicine, ensuring that the rest of your dog's life will be as long, active, happy and healthy as possible. If you do notice indications of aging, such as graying and/or changes in sleeping, eating or toileting habits, this is a sign to set up a senior-care visit with your vet right away to make sure that these changes are not related to any health problems.

To start, senior dogs should visit the vet twice yearly for exams, routine tests and overall evaluations. Many veterinarians have special screening programs especially for senior dogs that can include a thorough physical exam; blood test to determine complete blood count; serum biochemistry test, which screens for liver, kidney and blood problems as well as cancer; urinalysis; and dental exams. With these tests, it can be determined whether your dog has any health problems; the results also establish a baseline for your pet against which future test results can be compared.

In addition to these tests, your vet may suggest additional testing, including an EKG, tests for glaucoma and other problems of the eye, chest x-rays, screening for tumors, blood pressure test, test for thyroid function and screening for parasites and reassessment of his preventive program. Your vet also will ask you questions about your dog's diet and activity level, what you feed and the amounts that you feed. This information, along with his evaluation of the dog's overall condition, will enable him to suggest proper dietary changes, if needed.

This may seem like quite a work-up for your pet, but veterinarians advise that older dogs need more frequent attention so that any health problems can be

WEATHER WORRIES

Older pets are less tolerant of extremes in weather, both heat and cold. Your older dog should not spend extended periods in the sun; when outdoors in the warm weather, make sure he does not become overheated. In chilly weather, consider a sweater for your dog when outdoors and limit time spent outside. Whether or not his coat is thinning, he will need provisions to keep him warm when the weather is cold. You may even place his bed by a heating duct in your living room or bedroom.

detected as early as possible. Serious conditions like kidney disease, heart disease and cancer may not present outward symptoms, or the problem may go undetected if the symptoms are mistaken by owners as just part of the aging process.

There are some conditions more common in elderly dogs that are difficult to ignore. Cognitive dysfunction shares much in common with senility and Alzheimer's disease, and dogs are not immune. Dogs can become confused and/or disoriented, lose their house-training, have abnormal sleep-wake cycles and interact differently with their owners. Be heartened by the fact that, in some ways, there are more treatment options for dogs with cognitive dysfunction than for people with similar conditions. There is good evidence that continued stimulation in the form of games, play, training and exercise can help to maintain cognitive function. There are also medications (such as seligiline) and antioxidant-fortified senior diets that have been shown to be beneficial.

Cancer is also a condition more common in the elderly. Almost all of the cancers seen in people are also seen in pets. While we can't control the effects of second-hand smoke, lung cancer, which is a major killer in humans, is relatively rare in dogs. If pets are getting regular physical examinations, cancers are often detected early. There are a variety of cancer therapies available today, and many pets continue to live happy lives with appropriate treatment.

Degenerative joint disease, often referred to as arthritis, is another malady common to both elderly dogs and humans. A lifetime of wear and tear on joints and running around at play eventually take toll and result in stiffness and difficulty in getting around. As dogs live longer and healthier lives, it is natural that they should eventually feel some of the effects of aging. Once again, if regular veterinary care has been available, your pet was not carrying extra pounds all those years and wearing those joints out before their time. If your pet was unfortunate enough to inherit hip dysplasia, osteochondritis dissecans or any of the other developmental orthopedic diseases, battling the onset of degenerative joint disease was probably a longstanding goal. In any case, there are now many effective remedies for managing degenerative joint disease and a number of remarkable surgeries as well.

Aside from the extra veterinary care, there is much you can do at home to keep your older dog in good condition. The dog's diet is an important factor. If your dog's appetite decreases, he will not be getting the nutrients he needs. He also will lose weight, which is unhealthy for a dog at a proper weight. Conversely, an older dog's metabolism is slower and he usually exercises less, but he should not be allowed to become obese. Obesity in an older dog is especially risky, because extra pounds mean extra stress on the body, increasing his vulnerability to heart disease. Additionally, the extra pounds make it harder for the dog to move about.

You should discuss age-related feeding changes with your vet. For a dog who has lost interest in food, it may be suggested to try some different types of food until you find something new that the dog likes. For an obese dog, a "light"-formula dog food or reducing food portions may be advised, along with exercise appropriate to his physical condition and energy level.

As for exercise, the senior dog should not be allowed to become a "couch potato" despite his old age. He may not be able to handle the morning run, long walks and vigorous games of fetch, but he still needs to get up and get moving. Keep up with your daily walks, but keep the distances shorter and let your dog set the pace. If he gets to the point where he's not up for walks, let him stroll around the yard. On the other hand, many dogs remain very active in their senior years, so base changes to the exercise program on your own individual dog and what he's capable of. Don't worry, your Skye Terrier will let you know when it's time to rest.

Keep up with your grooming routine as you always have. Be extra diligent about checking the skin and coat for problems. Older dogs can experience thinning coats as a normal aging process, but they can also lose hair as a result of medical problems. Some thinning is normal, but patches of baldness or the loss of significant amounts of hair is not.

Hopefully, you've been regular with brushing your dog's teeth throughout his life. Healthy teeth directly affect overall good health. We already know that bacteria from gum infections can enter the dog's body through the damaged gums and travel to the organs. At a stage in life when his organs don't function as well as they used to, you don't want anything to put additional strain on them. Clean teeth also contribute to a healthy immune system. Offering the dental-type chews in addition to toothbrushing can help, as they remove plaque and tartar as the dog chews.

Along with the same good care you've given him all of his life, pay a little extra attention to your dog in his senior years and keep up with twice-yearly trips to the vet. The sooner a problem is uncovered, the greater the chances of a full recovery.

SHOWING YOUR SKYE TERRIER

Is dog showing in your blood? Are you excited by the idea of gaiting your handsome Skye Terrier around the ring to the thunderous applause of an enthusiastic audience? Are you certain that your beloved Skye Terrier is flawless? You are not alone! Every loving owner thinks that his dog has no faults, or too few to mention. No matter how many times an owner reads the breed standard, he cannot find any faults in his aristocratic companion dog. If this sounds like you, and if you are considering entering your Skye Terrier in a dog show, here are some basic questions to ask yourself:

- Did you purchase a "show-quality" puppy from the breeder?
- Is your puppy at least six months of age?
- Does the puppy exhibit correct show type for his breed?
- Does your puppy have any disqualifying faults?
- Is your Skye Terrier registered with the American Kennel Club?
- How much time do you have to devote to training, grooming, conditioning and exhibiting your dog?
- Do you understand the rules and regulations of a dog show?
- Do you have time to learn how to show your dog properly?
- Do you have the financial resources to invest in showing your dog?
- Will you show the dog yourself or hire a professional handler?
- Do you have a vehicle that can accommodate your weekend trips to the dog shows?

Success in the show ring requires more than a pretty face, a

SHOW POTENTIAL

How possible is it to predict how your ten-week-old puppy will eventually do in the show ring? Most show dogs reach their prime at around three years of age, when their bodies are physically mature and their coats are in "full bloom." Experienced breeders, having watched countless pups grow into Best of Breed winners, recognize the glowing attributes that spell "show potential." When selecting a puppy for show, it's best to trust the breeder to recommend which puppy will best suit your aspirations. Some breeders recommend starting with a male puppy, which likely will be more "typey" than his female counterpart.

SKYE TERRIER

The show world offers many challenges to Skye Terriers and their owners. Visit a dog show to get a real taste of the excitement and charisma of the show set.

waggy tail and a pocketful of liver. Even though dog shows can be exciting and enjoyable, the sport of conformation makes great demands on the exhibitors and the dogs. Winning exhibitors live for their dogs, devoting time and money to their dogs' presentation, conditioning and training. Very few novices, even those with good dogs, will find themselves in the winners' circle, though it does happen. Don't be disheartened, though. Every exhibitor began as a novice and worked his way up to the Group ring. It's the "working your way up" part that you must keep in mind.

Assuming that you have purchased a puppy of the correct type and quality for showing, let's begin to examine the world of showing and what's required to get started. Although the entry fee into a dog show is nominal,

AKC GROUPS
For showing purposes, the American Kennel Club divides its recognized breeds into seven groups: Terriers, Sporting Dogs, Hounds, Working Dogs, Toys, Non-Sporting Dogs and Herding Dogs.

there are lots of other hidden costs involved with "finishing" your Skye Terrier, that is, making him a champion. Things like equipment, travel, training and conditioning all cost money. A more serious campaign will include fees for a professional handler, boarding, cross-country travel and advertising. Top-winning show dogs can represent a very considerable investment—over $100,000 has been spent in campaigning some dogs. (The investment can be less, of course, for owners who don't use professional handlers.)

Many owners, on the other hand, enter their "average" Skye Terriers in dog shows for the fun and enjoyment of it. Dog showing makes an absorbing hobby, with many rewards for dogs and owners alike. If you're having fun, meeting other people who share your interests and enjoying the overall experience, you likely will catch the "bug." Once the dog-show bug bites, its effects can last a lifetime; it's certainly much better than a deer tick! Soon you will be envisioning yourself in the center ring at the Westminster Kennel Club Dog Show in New York City, competing for the prestigious Best in Show cup. This magical dog show is televised annually from Madison Square Garden, and the victorious dog becomes a celebrity overnight.

DRESS THE PART

It's a dog show, so don't forget your costume. Even though the show is about the dog, you also must play your role well. You have been cast as the "dog handler" and you must smartly dress the part. Solid colors make a nice complement to the dog's coat, but choose colors that contrast. You don't want to be wearing a solid color that blends mostly or entirely with the major or only color of your dog. Whether the show is indoors or out, you still must dress properly. You want the judge to perceive you as being professional, so polish, polish, polish! And don't forget to wear sensible shoes; remember, you have to gait around the ring with your dog.

Check out this Skye line! Although the dogs are lined up side-by-side, each Skye is compared to the breed standard and not the other entries.

AKC CONFORMATION SHOWING

Getting Started

Visiting a dog show as a spectator is a great place to start. Pick up the show catalog to find out what time your breed is being shown, who is judging the breed and in which ring the classes will be held. To start, Skye Terriers compete against other Skye Terriers, and the winner is selected as Best of Breed by the judge. This is the procedure for each breed. At a group show, all of the Best of Breed winners go on to compete for Group One in their respective group. For example, all Best of Breed winners in a given group compete against each other; this is done for all seven groups. Finally, all seven group winners

BECOMING A CHAMPION

An official AKC championship of record requires that a dog accumulate 15 points under three different judges, including two "majors" under different judges. Points are awarded based on the number of dogs entered into competition, varying from breed to breed and place to place. A win of three, four or five points is considered a "major." The AKC annually assigns a schedule of points to adjust for variations that accompany a breed's popularity and the population of a given area.

go head to head in the ring for the Best in Show award.

What most spectators don't understand is the basic idea of conformation. A dog show is often referred to as a "conformation" show. This means that the judge should decide how each dog stacks up (conforms) to the breed standard for his given breed: how well does this Skye Terrier conform to the ideal representative detailed in the standard? Ideally, this is what happens. In reality, however, this ideal often gets slighted as the judge compares Skye Terrier #1 to Skye Terrier #2. Again, the ideal is that each dog is judged based on his merits in comparison to his breed standard, not in comparison to the other dogs in the ring. It is easier for judges to compare dogs of the same breed to decide which they think is the better specimen; in the Group and Best in Show ring, however, it is very difficult to compare one breed to another, like apples to oranges. Thus the dog's conformation to the breed standard—not to mention advertising dollars and good handling—is essential to success in conformation shows. The dog described in the standard (the standard for each AKC breed is written and approved by the breed's national parent club and then submitted to the AKC for approval) is the perfect dog of that breed, and breeders keep their eyes on the standard when they choose which

MEETING THE IDEAL
The American Kennel Club defines a standard as: "A description of the ideal dog of each recognized breed, to serve as an ideal against which dogs are judged at shows." This "blueprint" is drawn up by the breed's recognized parent club, approved by a majority of its membership, and then submitted to the AKC for approval.

dogs to breed, hoping to get closer and closer to the ideal with each litter.

Another good first step for the novice is to join a dog club. You will be astonished by the many and different kinds of dog clubs in the country, with about 5,000 clubs holding events every year. Most clubs require that prospective new members present two letters of recommendation from existing members. Perhaps you've made some friends visiting a show held by a particular club and you would like to join that club. Dog clubs may specialize in a single breed, like a local or regional Skye Terrier club, or in a specific pursuit, such as obedience, tracking or hunting tests. There are all-breed clubs for all dog enthusiasts; they sponsor special training days, seminars on topics like grooming or handling or lectures on breeding or canine genetics. There are also clubs that specialize in certain types of dogs, like herding dogs, hunting dogs, companion dogs, etc.

A parent club is the national organization, sanctioned by the AKC, which promotes and safeguards its breed in the country. The Skye Terrier Club of America was formed in 1938 and can be contacted on the Internet at http://clubs.akc.org/skye/. The parent club holds an annual national specialty show, usually in a different city each year, in which many of the country's top dogs, handlers and breeders gather to compete. At a specialty show, only members of a single breed are invited to participate. There are also group specialties, in which all members of a group are invited. For more information about dog clubs in your area, contact the AKC at www.akc.org on the Internet or write them at their Raleigh, NC address.

OTHER TYPES OF COMPETITION

In addition to conformation shows, the AKC holds a variety of other competitive events. Obedience trials, agility trials and tracking trials are open to all breeds, while hunting tests, field trials, lure coursing, herding tests and trials, earthdog trials and coonhound events are limited to specific breeds or groups of breeds. The Junior Showmanship Program is offered to aspiring young handlers and their dogs, and the Canine Good Citizen® Program is an all-around good-behavior test open to all dogs, pure-bred and mixed.

Obedience Trials

Mrs. Helen Whitehouse Walker, a Standard Poodle fancier, can be credited with introducing obedience trials to the United States. In the 1930s she designed a series of exercises based on those of the Associated Sheep, Police, Army Dog Society of Great Britain. These exercises were intended to

> **WORKING TRIALS FOR TERRIERS**
>
> In the US, the American Working Terrier Association offers a Certificate of Gameness at sanctioned trials. A dog must enter a 3-meter-long tunnel buried in the ground, which includes one right-angle turn. Once in the tunnel, he must reach his prey in 30 seconds. Working trials are held throughout the country and are open to all terriers.

evaluate the working relationship between dog and owner. Since those early days of the sport in the US, obedience trials have grown more and more popular, and now more than 2,000 trials each year attract over 100,000 dogs and their owners. Any dog registered with the AKC, regardless of neutering or other disqualifications that would preclude entry in conformation competition, can participate in obedience trials.

There are three levels of difficulty in obedience competition. The first (and easiest) level is the Novice, in which dogs can earn the Companion Dog (CD) title. The intermediate level is the Open level, in which the Companion Dog Excellent (CDX) title is awarded. The advanced level is the Utility level, in which dogs compete for the Utility Dog (UD) title. Classes at each level are further divided into "A" and "B," with "A" for beginners and "B" for those with more experience. In order to win a title at a given level, a dog must earn three "legs." A "leg" is accomplished when a dog scores 170 or higher (200 is a perfect score). The scoring system gets a little trickier when you understand that a dog must score more than 50% of the points available for each exercise in order to actually earn the points. Available points for each exercise range between 20 and 40.

A dog must complete different exercises at each level of obedience. The Novice exercises are the easiest, with the Open and finally

The judge assesses this Skye Terrier competitor. A hands-on inspection is necessary in the conformation ring, especially for the Skye with its long coat. Looks can be deceiving.

MEET THE AKC

The American Kennel Club is the main governing body of the dog sport in the United States. Founded in 1884, the AKC consists of 500 or more independent dog clubs plus 4,500 affiliated clubs, all of which follow the AKC rules and regulations. Additionally, the AKC maintains a registry for pure-bred dogs in the US and works to preserve the integrity of the sport and its continuation in the country. Over 1,000,000 dogs are registered each year, representing about 150 recognized breeds. There are over 15,000 competitive events held annually for which over 2,000,000 dogs enter to participate. Dogs compete to earn over 40 different titles, from Champion to Companion Dog to Master Agility Champion.

I SMELL A WINNER
Tracking tests are exciting ways to test your Skye's instinctive scenting ability on a competitive level. All dogs have a nose, and all breeds are welcome in tracking tests. The first AKC-licensed tracking test took place in 1937 as part of the Utility level at an obedience trial, and thus competitive tracking was officially begun. The first title, Tracking Dog (TD), was offered in 1947, ten years after the first official tracking test. It was not until 1980 that the AKC added the title Tracking Dog Excellent (TDX), which was followed by the title Variable Surface Tracking (VST) in 1995. Champion Tracker (CT) is awarded to a dog who has earned all three of those titles.

level, the Novice-level exercises are required again, but this time without a leash and for longer durations. In addition, the dog must clear a broad jump, retrieve over a jump and drop on recall. In the Utility level, the exercises are quite difficult, including executing basic commands based on hand signals, following a complex heeling pattern, locating articles based on scent discrimination and completing jumps at the handler's direction.

Once he's earned the UD title, a dog can go on to win the prestigious title of Utility Dog Excellent (UDX) by winning "legs" in ten shows. Additionally, Utility Dogs who win "legs" in Open B and Utility B earn points toward the lofty title of Obedience Trial Champion (OTCh.). Established in 1977 by the AKC, this title requires a dog to earn 100 points as well as 3 first places in a combination of Open B and Utility B classes under 3 different judges. The "brass ring" of obedience competition is the AKC's National Obedience Invitational. This is an exclusive competition for only the cream of the obedience crop. In order to qualify for the invitational, a dog must be ranked in either the top 25 all-breeds in obedience or in the top 3 for his breed in obedience. The title at stake here is that of National Obedience Champion (NOC).

the Utility levels progressing in difficulty. Examples of Novice exercises are on- and off-lead heeling, a figure-8 pattern, performing a recall (or come), long sit and long down and standing for examination. In the Open

Showing

Showing your Skye Terrier is one of the great pleasures resulting from owning a fine-quality dog.

This is Lairdoglen Steel Magnolia shooting through the hoop, the first Skye Terrier to earn an agility title.

RALLY OBEDIENCE

In 2005 the AKC began a new program called rally obedience, and soon this exciting agility spin-off began sweeping the US. This is a less formal activity yet titles are awarded. There are four levels of competition. Novice, Advanced, Excellent and Advanced/Excellent. The dog and handler do a series of exercises designed by the judge and are timed. The handlers are encouraged to talk to their dogs as they work through the course. The judge evaluates each team on how well it executes one continuous performance over the whole course. The team works on its own as soon as the judge gives the order to begin. Handlers develop their own style in working with their dogs, using a combination of body language and hand signals as well as verbal commands. Faster and more accurate are desirable, though each team must work at its own pace. Signs are set up around the ring to indicate which exercise (or combination of exercises) is required. Working closely around the course, the team moves from one sign to the next, performing the various exercises. There are 50 exercises to choose from, varying in complexity and difficulty.

The dogs love this and it shows by their animation and energy. Many of the dogs who participate in obedience or agility also do well in rally. While most of the first rally titles have gone to seasoned obedience dogs, it's encouraging that some newcomers have also earned awards. Rally is a good way for a beginner to start out in obedience, and we hope that it will become a stepping stone to the obedience world and we will see many more dogs and owners coming into the ring.

AGILITY TRIALS

Agility trials became sanctioned by the AKC in August 1994, when the first licensed agility trials were held. Since that time, agility certainly has grown in popularity by leaps and bounds, literally! The AKC allows all registered breeds (including Miscellaneous Class breeds) to participate, providing the dog is 12 months of age or older. Agility is designed so that the handler demonstrates how well the dog can work at his side. The handler directs his dog through, over, under and around an obstacle course that includes jumps, tires, the dog walk, weave poles, pipe tunnels, collapsed tunnels and more. While working his way through the course, the dog must keep one eye and ear on the handler and the rest of his body on the course. The handler runs along with the dog, giving verbal and hand signals to guide the dog through the course.

The first organization to promote agility trials in the US was the United States Dog Agility Association, Inc. (USDAA). Established in 1986, the USDAA sparked the formation of many member clubs around the country. To participate in USDAA trials, dogs must be at least 18 months of age.

The USDAA and AKC both offer titles to winning dogs, although the exercises and requirements of the two organizations differ. Agility Dog (AD), Advanced Agility Dog (AAD) and Master Agility Dog (MAD) are the titles offered by the USDAA, while the AKC offers Novice Agility (NA), Open Agility (OA), Agility Excellent (AX) and Master Agility Excellent (MX). Beyond these four AKC titles, dogs can

Ch. Flambean's Mack the Knife, the number one Skye Terrier in 1990, shown by Denny Maurice, winning a terrier Group First under judge Margeret Young.

Show judges closely examine each Skye Terrier entered in competition, comparing it to the breed standard. The dog that conforms most closely to the standard, in the judge's estimation, is the winner.

various obstacles as well as training classes to prepare him for competition. In no time, your dog will be climbing A-frames, crossing the dog walk and flying over hurdles, all with you right beside him. Your heart will leap every time your dog jumps through the hoop—and you'll be having just as much (if not more) fun!

win additional titles in "jumper" classes: Jumper with Weave Novice (NAJ), Open (OAJ) and Excellent (MXJ). The ultimate title in AKC agility is MACH, Master Agility Champion. Dogs can continue to add number designations to the MACH title, indicating how many times the dog has met the title's requirements (MACH1, MACH2 and so on).

Agility trials are a great way to keep your dog active, and they will keep you running, too! You should join a local agility club to learn more about the sport. These clubs offer sessions in which you can introduce your dog to the

EARTHDOG EVENTS
Earthdog trials are held for those breeds that were developed to "go to ground." These dogs were bred to go down into badger and fox holes and bring out the quarry. Breeds such as Parson Russell Terriers, Dachshunds and other short-legged hunters are used in this fashion. Earthdog trials test the dog in a simulated hunting situation in which trenches are dug and lined, usually with wood. The scent of a rat is laid in the trench, and the quarry is a caged rat at the end of the tunnel. The dog can see and smell the rat but cannot touch or harm the quarry in any way.

There are four levels in earthdog trials. The first, Introduction to Quarry, is for beginners and uses a 10-foot tunnel. No title is awarded at this level. The Junior Earthdog (JE) title is awarded at the next level, which uses a 30-foot tunnel with three 90-degree turns. Two qualifying JE runs are required for a dog to earn the title. The next level, Senior Earthdog

(SE), uses the same length tunnel and number of turns as in the JE level, but also has a false den and exit and requires the dog to come out of the tunnel when called. To try for the SE title, a dog must have at least his JE; the SE title requires three qualifying runs at this level. The most difficult of the earthdog tests, Master Earthdog (ME), again uses the 30-foot tunnel with three 90-degree turns, with a false entrance, exit and den. The dog is required to enter in the right place and, in this test, honor another working dog. The ME title requires four qualifying runs, and a dog must have earned his SE title to attempt the ME level.

Best of Breed out of 78 Skyes competing at the Montgomery County Kennel Club in 2002, Ch. Seamist Joyful Noise with specialist judge Christine S. Crowell.

FOR MORE INFORMATION...
For reliable up-to-date information about registration, dog shows and other canine competitions, contact one of the national registries by mail or via the Internet.

American Kennel Club
5580 Centerview Dr., Raleigh, NC 27606-3390
www.akc.org

United Kennel Club
100 E. Kilgore Road, Kalamazoo, MI 49002
www.ukcdogs.com

Canadian Kennel Club
89 Skyway Ave., Suite 100, Etobicoke, Ontario M9W 6R4, Canada
www.ckc.ca

The Kennel Club
1-5 Clarges St., Piccadilly, London W1Y 8AB, UK
www.the-kennel-club.org.uk

CANINE FREESTYLE
One activity that is quickly gaining popularity and surely will have your dog wagging his tail, or in this case *shaking* his tail, is canine freestyle, or dog dancing. In freestyle a dog-and-handler team performs a choreographed dance routine to a musical composition of the team's choosing. This can be a fun and educational activity, as it incorporates traditional obedience training and allows the handler the freedom to integrate variations or invented steps and tricks that are not allowed in strict obedience showing. The dog and handler often

At the Montgomery County Kennel Club All-Terrier Show in 2003, the Best of Breed Skye Terrier was Ch. Here's Pandora of Morningsky under judge Gary Vlachos.

dress in a style suited to the piece of music they have selected.

It is important that the dog's trainer be quite dedicated and skilled, as some breeds of dog are more difficult to train than others. Also, some moves in freestyle can put strain on the dog's joints, so be sure the dog is fully developed and in good health before beginning his dance regimen.

If freestyle seems to be an activity you and your Skye Terrier might be interested in, there are various organizations that hold freestyle shows. One such organization is the World Canine Freestyle Organization (WCFO), founded in 1999 by Patie Ventre. The WCFO holds numerous freestyle events each year, providing an opportunity for dogs to earn titles. There are member clubs throughout the United States, and more information can be found at the WCFO's website: www.worldcaninefreestyle.org.

CANINE GOOD CITIZEN® PROGRAM

Have you ever considered getting your dog "certified"? The AKC's Canine Good Citizen® Program affords your dog just that opportunity. Your dog shows that he is a well-behaved canine citizen, using the basic training and good manners you have taught him, by taking a series of ten tests that illustrate that he can behave properly at home, in a public place and around other dogs. The tests are administered by participating dog clubs, colleges, 4-H clubs, Scouts and other community groups and are open to all pure-bred and mixed-breed dogs. Upon passing the ten tests, the suffix CGC is then applied to your dog's name.

The ten tests are: 1. Accepting a friendly stranger; 2. Sitting politely for petting; 3. Appearance and grooming; 4. Walking on a lead; 5. Walking through a group of people; 6. Sit, down and stay on command; 7. Coming when called; 8. Meeting another dog; 9. Calm reaction to distractions; 10. Separation from owner.

BEHAVIOR OF YOUR SKYE TERRIER

As a Skye Terrier owner, you have selected your dog so that you and your loved ones can have a companion, a protector, a friend and a four-legged family member. You invest time, money and effort to care for and train the family's new charge. Of course, this chosen canine behaves perfectly! Well, perfectly like a *dog*.

THINK LIKE A DOG
Dogs do not think like humans, nor do humans think like dogs, though we try. Unfortunately, a dog is incapable of comprehending how humans think, so the responsibility falls on the owner to adopt a proper canine mindset. Dogs cannot rationalize, and they exist in the present moment. Many dog owners make the mistake in training of thinking that they can reprimand their dog for something he did a while ago. Basically, you cannot even reprimand a dog for something he did 20 seconds ago. Either catch him in the act or forget it. It is a waste of your and your dog's time—in his mind, you are reprimanding him for whatever he is doing at that moment.

The following behavioral problems represent some which owners most commonly encounter. Every dog is unique and every situation is unique. No author could describe to you how to solve your Skye's problems simply by writing it down. Here we outline some basic "dogspeak" so that owners' chances of solving behavioral problems are increased.

Discuss bad habits with your veterinarian, and he can recommend a behavioral specialist to consult in appropriate cases. Since behavioral abnormalities are the main reason for owners' abandoning their pets, we hope that you will make a valiant effort to solve your Skye's problems. Patience and understanding are virtues that must dwell in every pet-loving household.

SEPARATION ANXIETY
Any behaviorist will tell you that separation anxiety is the most common problem about which pet owners complain. It is also one of the easiest to prevent. Unfortunately, a behaviorist usually is not consulted until the dog is a stressed-out, neurotic

mess. At that stage, it is indeed a problem that requires the help of a professional.

> **EXIT STAGE LEFT**
> Your dog studies your every move. He knows that before you leave the house you gather a bunch of stuff, put on your coat and shake your keys. His anxiety emerges at the first sight of seeing you begin your "exit routine." If your dog suffers from separation anxiety, you should rethink your exit. Mix up your routine and include your dog in some of the tasks. Play a short game of fetch, reward the dog for correct responses to a couple of commands, present him with a safe toy and give him a treat before you leave the house. If the dog is exercised, content and focused on something other than your exit, he may learn to adapt better to your absence.

Training the puppy to the fact that people in the house come and go is essential in order to avoid this anxiety. Leaving the puppy in his crate or a confined area while family members go in and out, and stay out for longer and longer periods of time, is the basic way to desensitize the pup to the family's frequent departures. If you are at home most of every day, make it a point to go out for at least an hour or two whenever possible.

How you leave is vital to the dog's reaction. Your dog is no fool. He knows the difference between sweats and business suits, jeans and dresses. He sees you pat your pocket to check for your wallet, open your briefcase, check that you have your cell phone or pick up the car keys. He knows from the hurry of the kids in the morning that they're off to school until afternoon. Lipstick? Aftershave lotion? Lunch boxes? Every move you make registers in his sensory perception and memory. Your puppy knows more about your departures than you do. You can't get away with a thing!

Before you got dressed, you checked the dog's water bowl and his supply of toys (including a long-lasting chew toy) and turned the radio on low. You will leave him in what he considers his "safe" area, not with total freedom of the house. If you've invested in

The Skye left alone most of the time might develop separation anxiety, a syndrome which may result in destructive behavior.

child safety gates, you can be reasonably sure that he'll remain in the designated area. Don't give him access to a window where he can watch you leave the house. If you're leaving for an hour or two, just put him into his crate with a safe toy.

Now comes the test! You are ready to walk out the door. Do not give your Skye Terrier a big hug and a fond farewell. Do not drag out a long goodbye. Those are the very things that jump-start separation anxiety. Toss a biscuit into the dog's area, call out "So long, pooch" and close the door. You're gone. The chances are that the dog may bark a couple of times, or maybe whine once or twice, and then settle down to enjoy his biscuit and take a lovely nap, especially if you took him for a nice long walk after breakfast. As he grows up, the barks and whines will stop because it's an

One of the best treatments for separation anxiety is a second Skye Terrier. Dogs feel more secure in the company of other canines.

old routine, so why should he make the effort?

When you first brought home the puppy, the come-and-go routine was intermittent and constant. He was put into his crate with a tiny treat. You left (silently) and returned in 3 minutes, then 5, then 10, then 15, then half an hour, until finally you could leave without a problem and be gone for 2 or 3 hours. If, at any time in the future, there's a "separation" problem, refresh his memory by going back to that basic training.

Now comes the next most important part—your return. Do not make a big production of coming home. "Hi, poochie" is as grand a greeting as he needs. When you've taken off your hat and coat, tossed your briefcase on the hall table and glanced at the mail, and the dog has settled down from the excitement of seeing you "in person" from his confined area, then go and give him a warm, friendly greeting. A potty trip is needed and a walk would be appreciated, since he's been such a good dog.

AGGRESSION
"Aggression" is a word that is often misunderstood and is sometimes even used to describe

I CAN'T SMILE WITHOUT YOU

How can you tell whether your dog is suffering from separation anxiety? Not every dog who enjoys a close bond with his owner will suffer from separation anxiety. In actuality, only a small percentage of dogs are affected. Separation anxiety manifests itself in dogs older than one year of age and may not occur until the dog is a senior. A number of destructive behaviors are associated with the problem, including scratch marks in front of doorways, bite marks on furniture, drool stains on furniture and flooring and tattered draperies, carpets or cushions. The most reliable sign of separation anxiety is howling and crying when the owner leaves and then barking like mad for extended periods. Affected dogs may also defecate or urinate throughout the home, attempt to escape when the door opens, vocalize excessively and show signs of depression (including loss of appetite, listlessness and lack of activity).

what is actually normal canine behavior. For example, it's normal for puppies to growl when playing tug-of-war. It's puppy talk. There are different forms of dog aggression, but all are degrees of dominance, indicating that the dog, not his master, is (or thinks he is) in control. When the dog feels that he (or his control of the situation) is threatened, he will respond. The extent of the aggressive behavior varies with individual dogs. It is not at all pleasant to see bared teeth or to hear your dog growl or snarl, but these are signs of behavior that, if left uncorrected, can become extremely dangerous. A word of warning here: never challenge an aggressive dog. He is unpredictable and therefore unreliable to approach.

Nothing gets a "hello" from strangers on the street quicker than walking a puppy, but people should ask permission before petting your dog so you can tell him to sit in order to receive the admiring pats. If a hand comes down over the dog's head and he shrinks back, ask the person to bring their hand up, underneath the pup's chin. Now you're correcting strangers, too! But if you don't, it could make your dog afraid of strangers, which in turn can lead to fear biting. Socialization prevents much aggression before it rears its ugly head.

"DOG" SPOKEN HERE

Dogs' verbal language is limited to four words: growl, bark, whine and howl. Their body language is what tells the tale. They communicate with each other, and hopefully with you, through precise postures. You know what the friendly wagging tail and the play-bow (down in front, up in rear) mean, but there's many other things that you can decipher from your dog's body language. When the dog turns belly up, or on his side with one leg raised, he's being totally submissive. Looking away (breaking eye contact) and laid-back ears are other signs of submission. With ears at attention, mouth open and tail in a neutral position, the dog is watchful but relaxed. Fear is indicated by a crouching, even trembling, posture, with ears back, tail down and eyes averted. The aggressive dog attempts to look as large as possible to his adversary. He stalks stiffly, with his tail up, head high, ears alert, hackles raised, chest puffed out and lips curled, and with a stare that is cold and hard.

The body language of an aggressive dog about to attack is clear. The dog will have a hard, steady stare. He will try to look as big as possible by standing stiff-legged, pushing out his chest, keeping his ears up and holding his tail up and steady. The hackles on his back will rise so that a ridge of hairs stands up. This posture may include the curled lip, snarl and/or growl, or he may be silent. He looks, and definitely is, very dangerous.

This dominant posture is seen in dogs that are territorially aggressive. Deliverymen are constant victims of serious bites from such dogs. Territorial aggression is the reason you should never, ever try to train a puppy to be a watchdog. It can escalate into this type of behavior over which you will have no control. All forms of aggression must be taken seriously and dealt with immediately. If signs of aggressive behavior continue, or grow worse, or if you are at all unsure about how to deal with your dog's behavior, get the help of a professional.

Uncontrolled aggression, sometimes called "irritable aggression," is not something for the pet owner to try to solve. If you cannot solve your dog's dangerous behavior with professional help, and you (quite rightly) do not wish to keep a canine time-bomb in your home, you will have some important decisions to make. Aggressive dogs often cannot be rehomed successfully, as they are dangerous and unreliable in their behavior. An aggressive dog should be dealt with only by someone who knows exactly the situation that he is getting into and has the experience, dedication and ideal living environment

THE MACHO DOG

The Venus/Mars differences are found in dogs, too. Males have distinct behaviors that, while seemingly sex-related, are more closely connected to the role of the male as leader. Marking territory by urinating on it is one means that male dogs use to establish their presence. Doing so merely says, "I've been here." Small dogs often attempt to lift their legs higher on the tree than the previous male. While this is natural behavior outdoors on items like telephone poles, fence posts, fire hydrants and most other upright objects, marking indoors is totally unacceptable. Treat it as you would a house-training accident and clean thoroughly to eradicate the scent.

Another behavior often seen in the macho male, mounting is a dominance display. Neutering the dog before six months of age helps to deter this behavior. You can discourage him from mounting by catching the dog as he's about to mount you, stepping quickly aside and saying "Off!"

to attempt rehabilitating the dog, which often is not possible. In these cases, the dog ends up having to be humanely put down. Making a decision about euthanasia is not an easy undertaking for anyone, for any reason, but you cannot pass on to another home a dog that you know could cause harm.

A milder form of aggression is the dog's guarding anything that he perceives to be his—his food dish, his toys, his bed and/or his crate. This can be prevented if you take firm control from the start. The young puppy can and should be taught that his leader will share, but that certain rules apply. Guarding is mild aggression only in the beginning stages, and it will worsen and become dangerous if you let it.

Don't try to snatch anything away from your puppy. Bargain for the item in question so that you can positively reinforce him when he gives it up. Punishment only results in worsening any aggressive behavior.

Many dogs extend their guarding impulse toward items they've stolen. The dog figures, "If I have it, it's mine!" (Some ill-behaved kids have similar tendencies.) An angry confrontation will only increase the dog's aggression. (Have you ever watched a child have a tantrum?) Try a simple distraction first, such as tossing a toy or picking up his leash for a

THE TOP-DOG TUG

When puppies play tug-of-war, the dominant pup wins. Children also play this kind of game but, for their own safety, must be prevented from ever engaging in this type of play with their dogs. Playing tug-of-war games can result in a dog's developing aggressive behavior. Don't be the cause of such behavior.

walk. If that doesn't work, the best way to handle the situation is with basic obedience. Show the dog a treat, followed by calm, almost slow-motion commands: "Come. Sit. Drop it. Good dog," and then hand over the cheese. That's one example of positive-reinforcement training.

Children can be bitten when they try to retrieve a stolen shoe or toy, so they need to know how to handle the dog or to let an adult do it. They may also be bitten as they run away from a dog, in either fear or play. The dog sees the child's running as reason for pursuit, and even a friendly young puppy will nip at the heels of a runaway. Teach the kids not to run away from a strange dog and when to stop overly exciting play with their own puppy.

Fear biting is yet another aggressive behavior. A fear biter gives many warning signals. The dog leans away from the approaching person (sometimes hiding behind his owner) with his ears and tail down, but not in submission. He may even shiver. His hackles are raised, his lips curled. When the person steps into the dog's "flight zone" (a circle of 1 to 3 feet surrounding the dog), he attacks. Because of the fear factor, he performs a rapid attack-and-retreat. Because it is directed at a person, vets are often the victims of this form of aggression. It is frightening, but discovering and eliminating the cause of the fright will help overcome the dog's need to bite. Early socialization again plays a strong role in the prevention of this behavior. Again, if you can't cope with it, get the help of an expert.

MATTERS OF SEX
For whatever reasons, real or imagined, most people tend to have a preference in choosing between a male and female puppy. Some, but not all, of the undesirable traits attributed to the sex of the dog can be suppressed by early spaying or neutering. The major advantage, of course, is that a neutered male or a spayed female will not be adding to the overpopulation of dogs.

An unaltered male will mark territory by lifting his leg everywhere, leaving a few drops of urine indoors on your furniture and appliances, and outside on everything he passes. It is difficult to catch him in the act, because he leaves only a few drops each time, but it is very hard to eliminate the odor. Thus the cycle begins, because the odor will entice him to mark that spot again.

If you have bought a bitch with the intention of breeding her, be sure you know what you are getting into. She will go through one or two periods of estrus each year, each cycle lasting about three weeks. During those times she will have to be kept confined to protect your furniture and to protect her from being bred by a male other than the one you have selected. Breeding should never be undertaken to "show the kids the miracle of birth." Bitches can die giving birth, and the puppies may also die. The dam often exhibits what is called "maternal aggression" after the pups are born. Her intention is to protect her pups, but in fact she can be extremely vicious. Breeding should be left to the experienced breeders, who do so for the better-

> **GET A WHIFF OF HIM!**
> Dogs sniff each others' rears as their way of saying "Hi" as well as to find out who the other dog is and how he's doing. That's normal behavior between canines, but it can, annoyingly, extend to people. The command for all unwanted sniffing is "Leave it!" Give the command in a no-nonsense voice and move on.

ment of the breed and with much research and planning behind each mating.

Mounting is not unusual in dogs, male or female. Puppies do it to each other and adults do it regardless of sex, because it is not so much a sexual act as it is one of dominance. It becomes very annoying when the dog mounts your legs, the kids or the couch cushions; in these and any other instances of mounting, he should be corrected. Touching sometimes stimulates the dog, so pulling the dog off by his collar or leash, together with a consistent and stern "Off!" command, usually eliminates the behavior.

CHEWING

The national canine pastime is chewing, and Skyes have great big teeth to keep sharp and busy!

All puppies chew. All dogs chew. This is a fact of life for canines, and sometimes you may think it's what your dog does best! A pup starts chewing when his first set of teeth erupts and continues throughout the teething period. Chewing gives the pup relief from itchy gums and incoming teeth and, from that time on, he gets great satisfaction out of this normal, somewhat idle, canine activity. Providing safe chew toys is the best way to direct this behavior in an appropriate manner. Chew toys are available in all sizes, textures and flavors,

> **"LEAVE IT"**
> Watch your puppy like a hawk to be certain it's a toy he's chewing, not your wallet. When you catch him in the act, tell him "Leave it!" and substitute a proper toy. Chewing on anything other than his own safe toys is countered by spraying the desirable (to the dog) object with a foul-tasting product like Bitter Apple® and being more diligent in your observations of his chewing habits. When you can't supervise, it's crate time for Fido.

but you must monitor the wear-and-tear inflicted on your pup's toys to be sure that the ones you've chosen are safe and remain in good condition.

Puppies cannot distinguish between a rawhide toy and a nice leather shoe or wallet. It's up to you to keep your possessions away from the dog and to keep your eye on the dog. There's a form of destruction caused by chewing that is not the dog's fault. Let's say you allow him on the sofa. One day he takes a rawhide bone up on the sofa and, in the course of chewing on the bone, takes up a bit of fabric. He continues to chew. Disaster! Now you've learned the lesson: Dogs with chew toys have to be either kept off furniture and carpets, carefully supervised or put into their confined areas for chew time.

SKYE TERRIER

Every Skye's personality is different. Generalizations can be made about the breed's overall temperament, but each dog is an individual with his own likes and dislikes.

The wooden legs of furniture are favorite objects for chewing. The first time, tell the dog "Leave it!" (or "No!") and offer him a chew toy as a substitute. But your clever dog may be hiding under the chair and doing some silent destruction, which you may not notice until it's too late. In this case, it's time to try one of the foul-tasting, spray-on products, made specifically to prevent destructive chewing. These products also work to keep the dog away from plants, trash, etc. It's even a good way to stop the dog from "mouthing" or chewing on your hands or the leg of your pants. (Be sure to wash your hands after the mouthing lesson!) A little spray goes a long way.

DIGGING

Digging, which is seen as a destructive behavior to humans, is actually quite a natural behavior in dogs, especially in terrier breeds, who were created to dig! Terriers, of course, were bred to dig for purposeful reasons and not just wherever and whenever the dog wants. Any dog's desire to dig can be irrepressible and most frustrating to his owners.

Digging is another natural and normal doggie behavior. Wild canines dig to bury whatever food they can save for later to eat. (And you thought we invented the doggie bag!) Burying bones or toys is a primary cause to dig. Dogs also dig to get at interesting little underground creatures like moles and mice. In the summer, they dig to get down to cool earth. In

PROFESSIONAL HELP
Every trainer and behaviorist asks, "Why didn't you come to me sooner?" Pet owners often don't want to admit that anything is wrong with their dogs. A dog's problem often is due to the dog and his owner mixing their messages, which will only get worse. Don't put it off; consult a professional to find out whether or not the problem is serious enough to require intervention.

Behavior

winter, they dig to get beneath the cold surface to warmer earth.

The solution to the last two is easy. In the summer, provide a bed that's up off the ground and placed in a shaded area. In winter, the dog should either be indoors to sleep or given an adequate insulated doghouse outdoors. To understand how natural and normal this is you have only to consider the Nordic breeds of sled dog who, at the end of the run, routinely dig a bed for themselves in the snow. It's the nesting instinct. How often have you seen your dog go round and round in circles, pawing at his blanket or bedding before flopping down to sleep?

Domesticated dogs also dig to escape, and that's a lot more dangerous than it is destructive. A dog that digs under the fence is the one that is hit by a car or becomes lost. A good fence to protect a digger should be set 10 to 12 inches below ground level, and every fence needs to be routinely checked for even the smallest openings that can become possible escape routes.

Catching your dog in the act of digging is the easiest way to stop it, because your dog will make the "one-plus-one" connection, but digging is too often a solitary occupation, something the lonely dog does out of boredom. Catch your young puppy in the act and put a stop to it before you have a yard full of craters. It is more difficult to stop if your dog sees you gardening. If you can dig, why can't he? Because you say so, that's why! Some dogs are excavation experts, and some dogs never dig. However, when it comes to any of these instinctive canine behaviors, never say "never."

> **CURES FOR COMMON BOREDOM**
>
> Dogs are social animals that need company. Lonely and tied-out dogs bark, hoping that someone will hear them. Prevent this from happening by never tying your dog out in the yard and giving him the attention that he needs. If you don't, then don't blame the dog. Bored dogs will think up clever ways to overcome their boredom. Digging is a common diversion for a dog left alone outside for too long. The remedy is to bring him indoors or put a layer of crushed stone in his confined outdoor area. If you catch him in the act of "gardening," it requires immediate correction. Keep your dog safe by embedding the fencing a foot or more below ground level to foil a would-be escape artist.

JUMPING UP

Jumping up is a device of enthusiastic, attention-seeking puppies, but adult dogs often like to jump up as well, usually as a form of canine greeting. This is a controversial issue. Some owners wouldn't have it any other way! They encourage their dogs, and the owners and dogs alike enjoy the friendly physical contact. Some owners think that it's cute when it comes from a puppy, but not from an adult.

Conversely, there are those who consider jumping up to be one of the worst kinds of bad manners to be found in a dog. Among this group inevitably are bound to be some of your best friends. There are two situations in which your dog should be restrained from any and all jumping up. One is around children, especially young children and those who are not at ease with dogs. The other is when you are entertaining guests. No one who comes dressed up for a party wants to be groped by your dog, no matter how friendly his intentions or how clean his paws.

The answer to this one is relatively simple. If the dog has already started to jump up, the first command is "Off," followed immediately by "Sit." The dog must sit every time you are about to meet a friend on the street or when someone enters your home, be it child or adult. You may have to ask people to ignore the dog for a few minutes in order to let his urge for an enthusiastic greeting subside. If your dog is too exuberant and won't sit still, you'll have to work harder by first telling him "Off" and then issuing the down-stay command. This requires more work on your part, because the down is a submissive position and your dog is only trying to be super-friendly. A small treat is expected when training for this particular down.

If you have a real pet peeve about a dog's jumping up, then disallow it from the day your puppy comes home. Jumping up is a subliminally taught human-to-dog greeting. Dogs don't greet each other in this way. It begins because your puppy is close to the ground and he's easier to pet and cuddle if he reaches up and you bend over to meet him halfway. If you won't like it later, don't start it when he is young, but do give lots of praise and affection for a good sit.

BARKING
The Skye is not associated with the illustrious group of yappy terriers, thankfully! Skyes, alert and intelligent, tend to use their "big-dog" barks with great purpose.

However, there will be times when you will need to quite your Skye. Telling a dog he must not bark is like telling a child not to speak! Consider how confusing it must be to your dog that you are using your voice (which is your form of barking) to teach him when to bark and when not to! That is precisely the reason not to "bark back" when the dog's barking is annoying you (or your neighbors). Try to understand the scenario from the dog's viewpoint. He barks. You bark. He barks again, you bark again. This "conversation" can go on forever!

The first time your adorable little puppy said "Yip" or "Yap," you were ecstatic. His first word! You smiled, you told him how smart he was—and you allowed him to do it. So there's that one-plus-one thing again, because he will understand by your happy reaction that "Mr. Alpha loves it when I talk." Ignore his barking in the beginning, and allow it, but don't encourage barking during play. Instead, use the "put a toy in it" method to tone it down. Add a very soft "Quiet" as you hand off the toy. If the barking continues, stand up straight, fold your arms and turn your back on the dog. If he barks, you won't play, and you should follow the same rule for all undesirable behavior during play.

Dogs bark in reaction to sounds and sights. Another dog's bark, a person passing by or even just rustling leaves can set off a barker. If someone coming up your driveway or to your door provokes a barking frenzy, use the saturation method to stop it. Have several friends come and go every three or four minutes over as long a period of time as they can spare (it could take a couple of hours). Attach about a foot of rope to the dog's collar and have very small treats handy. Each time a car pulls up or a person approaches, let the dog bark once (grab the rope if you need to physically restrain him), say "Okay, good dog," give him a treat and make him sit. "Okay" is the release command. It lets the dog know that he has alerted you and tells him that you are now in charge. That person leaves and the next arrives and so on and so on until everyone—especially the dog—is bored and the barking has stopped. Don't forget to thank your friends. Your neighbors, by the way, may be more than willing to assist you in this parlor game.

Excessive barking outdoors is more difficult to keep in check

> **DID YOU HEAR THAT?**
> Dogs can lead you to think that they are the best watchdogs in the world when they're only barking at falling leaves or twinkling stars! (In which case, you should bring them indoors!) Dogs bark when they have nothing else to do. (In which case, they need appropriate distractions.) They continue to bark if, when they did it the first time, you reacted as if you thought it was cute. (Don't encourage them!) Dogs bark as they sit in the window, watching the world go by. (Draw the blinds!) Your dog needs to learn that one bark is all it takes to alert you. That's enough.

because, when it happens, he is outside and you are probably inside. A few warning barks are fine, but use the same method to tell him when enough is enough. You will have to stay outside with him for that bit of training.

There is one more kind of vocalizing which is called "idiot barking" (from idiopathic, meaning of unknown cause). It is usually rhythmic or a timed series of barks. Put a stop to it immediately by calling the dog to come. This form of barking can drive neighbors crazy and commonly occurs when a dog is left outside at night or for long periods of time during the day. He is completely and thoroughly bored! A change of scenery may help, such as relocating him to a room indoors when he is used to being outside. A few new toys or different dog biscuits might be the solution. If he is left alone and no one can get home during the day, a noontime walk with a local dog-sitter would be the perfect solution.

FOOD-RELATED PROBLEMS
We're not talking about eating, diets or nutrition here, we're talking about bad habits. Face it. All dogs are beggars. Food is the motivation for everything we want our dogs to do and, when you combine that with their innate ability to "con" us in order to get their way, it's a wonder there aren't far more obese dogs in the world.

Who can resist the bleeding-heart look that says "I'm starving," the paw that gently pats your knee and gives you a knowing look, the whining "please" or even the total body language of a perfect sit beneath the cookie jar. No one who professes to love his dog can turn down the pleas of his clever canine's performances every time. One thing is for sure, though: definitely do not allow begging at the table. Family meals do not include your dog.

Control your dog's begging habit by making your dog work

Skyes look up to their master for encouragement and instruction. If your Skye is exhibiting inappropriate behavior, it is wise to consult a specialist before the problem becomes too much for you to handle.

for his rewards. Ignore his begging when you can. Utilize the obedience commands you've taught your dog. Use "Off" for the pawing. A sit or even a long down will interrupt the whining. His reward in these situations is definitely not a treat! Casual verbal praise is enough. Be sure all members of the family follow the same rules. There is a different type of begging that does demand your immediate response and that is the appeal to be let (or taken) outside. Usually that is a quick paw or small whine to get your attention, followed by a race to the door. This type of begging needs your quick attention and approval. Of course, a really smart dog will soon figure out how to cut you off at the pass and direct you to that cookie jar on your way to the door. Some dogs are always one step ahead of us.

Stealing food is a problem only if you are not paying attention. A dog can't steal food that is not within his reach. Leaving your dog in the kitchen with the roast beef on the table is asking for trouble. Nothing idiopathic about this problem, though perhaps a little idiotic! Putting cheese and crackers on the coffee table also requires a watchful eye to stop the thief in his tracks. The word to use (one word, remember, even if it's two words pronounced as one) is "Leave it!" Instead of preceding it with yet another "No," try using a guttural sound like "Aagh!" That sounds more like a warning growl to the dog and therefore has instant meaning.

Canine thieves are in their element when little kids are carrying cookies in their hands. Your dog will think he's been exceptionally clever if he causes a child to drop a cookie. Bonanza! The easiest solution is to keep dog and children separated at snack time. You must also be sure that the children understand that they must not tease the dog with food—his or theirs. Your dog does not mean to bite the kids, but when he snatches at a tidbit so near the level of his mouth, it can result in an unintended nip.

Who can resist this delightful twosome? Never give in to begging Skyes.

INDEX

*Page numbers in **boldface** indicate illustrations.*

Acetaminophen 44
Activity level 58
—senior dog 126
Adenovirus 100
Adult dog
—adoption 72
—coat 59
—feeding 55
—health 95
—training 70, 72
Age 75
Aggression 48, 72, 86-87, 102, 144-145, 147
—maternal 38
Agility 90
—trials 132, 136
Aging 97
—signs of 121
Albatross of Skyeline **21**
Alexander, Miss 12
Alexandria, Queen 10
Alpha of Morningsky's 20
Alpha role 80
Amann, Mrs. J. Jay 18
American Heartworm Society 117
American Kennel Club 17, 127, 132-133, 140
—address 139
—competitive events 132
—conformation showing 130
American Working Terrier Association 132
Ancylostoma caninum **113**, 116
Antifreeze 42, 98
Antoinette, Marie 19
Appetite loss 98
Armadale Castle 9
Arreton kennels 13
Arthritis 125
Ascarid **112**, 113
Ascaris lumbricoides **112**
Attention 81, 83, 88, 151
Austria 19
Auto-immune disease 25
Barking 152-153
Bathing 60
Bedding 37, 45, 77
Behavior
—problems 141, 150
—senior dog 122
—specialist 141, 148
Behaviorist 150
Belgium 20
Best in Show 131
Best of Breed 130
Bite 32
Biting 86, 147
Bloat 98
Body language 73, 79, 84, 145-146, 154
Body type 22
Bones 38, 53
Bordetella 100
Bordetella bronchiseptica 101
Boredom 58, 151, 153
Borrelia burgdorferi 100
Borreliosis 101
Boucher, Bob and Anne 18
Bowls 35
Bracadale Henry 14-15
Bracadale Tiggy of Iradell 14
Breed club 31, 34, 91
Breed standard 26, 131
—differences between UK and US 22
Breeder 25, 26, 30-32, 34, 131
—selection 30, 33, 93
Brilliant Brisk of the Isle of Skye 21
Britain 9
Brown, Don and Anne 18
Brown, Jr., Charles 17

Brown, Tim and Diane 19
Brushing 59
Cairn Terrier 22
Caius, Dr. J. 12
Canadian Kennel Club
—address 139
Cancer 102, 120, 125
—breast 24
Canine cough 100
Canine development schedule 75
Canine Good Citizen® 132, 140
Car travel 46, 87
Cecilia, Crown Princess 19
Certificate of Gameness 132
Chamart, Madame 17
Champion Tracker 134
Chew toys 38-39, 41, 51, 76, 78, 149
Chewing 37, 41, 49, 87, 149
Cheyletiella mite **109**
Chiggers 111
Children 44, 47, 50, 72, 76, 87, 147, 152, 155
Choosing a Dog for Life 23
Cimarron Czigana v d Litsberg, **21**
Cimarron kennels 17
Cimarron Sarason Andrew 17
Clarkson Earl, Jr., Mrs. N. 13
Clicker training 91
Clubs 131
Coat 22, 58
—senior dog 126
Cognitive dysfunction 97, 123, 125
Cold weather 124
Collars 40 81, 87
Combing 59
Come 87
Command 83-90
—potty 77
—practicing 84, 86
Commitment of ownership 31, 33-34
Companion Dog 133
Companion Dog Excellent 133
Conformation showing 127-132
Consistency 47, 49-50, 72, 81
Core vaccines 101
Coronavirus 100-101
Correction 81
Crate 36, 45, 51, 76, 142, 149
—pads 37
—training 37, 79
Crook, Marion von Feldmahr 11
Crown Prince Charles of Meerend 19
Crying 45, 51, 77
Ctenocephalides canis **104**
Cuthbert, Mrs. 12
Czechoslovakia 19, 20
Dale, B. Nolan and Donna 17, 19
Dandie Dinmont 12
Dangers in the home 41-42
DEET 111
Degenerative joint disease 125
Demodex mite **111**
Demodicosis 110-111
Denmark 20
Dental care 95, 97, 98, 126
De Prisco, Andrew 23
Destructive behavior 58, 144, 150-151
Dewey, Jr., Mrs. Charles S. 15
Diana **12**
Diet 53
—adult 55
—puppy 52
—senior dog 56, 125
Digging 150-151
Dillis, Frau 19
Dipylidium caninum 114, **116**
Dirofilaria immitis 115, **116, 117**

Discipline 23, 49, 80
Disk disease 25
Distemper 100-101
Dog clubs 34, 132
Dogfight 87
Dominance 35, 84, 145-147, 149
Donaldson, George William 12
Down 78, 84
Down/stay 86, 152
Druidmoor kennels 17
Dry bath 60
Dunvegan Tail Toddle **15**
Eaden, Mrs. Harold 12
Ears
—cleaning 66
—drop and prick 10, 16
—mite infestation 66, 109-110
Earthdog trials 91, 132, 137
Echinococcus multilocularis 115
Eggs 53
Emergency care 98
Englishe Dogges 12
Escaping 151
Estrus 102, 148
Europe 19
Evening Star de Luchar 16
Excessive thirst 57
Exercise 57
—pen 76
—senior dog 126
Expenses of ownership 42
External parasites 104-111
Eye care 67
Eyesight 22
Family dog 23
Family meeting the puppy 44
Faygate kennels 12
Fear 48, 145
—aggression 86
—biting 145, 147
Fear period 47
Feeding 52-56
—adult 55-56
—puppy 52-54
—schedule 54
Fenced yard 24, 42, 87, 151
Finland 20
Finnish Skye Terrier Club 20
Finnsky kennels 20
First aid 98
First night in new home 45
Flambean's Mack the Knife **137**
Fleas **104**, 105, **106**
Food 53, 76
—bowls 35
—lack of interest in 98
—raw 53
—rewards 71, 81, 89
—stealing 155
—types of 52
France 20
Free-feeding 55
Genetic testing 93
Germany 19
Getting started in showing 130
Giardia 100
Glamoor Gang Buster 17, 18
Glamoor Go Go Go. 16
Glamoor Going Up 16
Glamoor Good News 16
Glamoor kennels 15, 17
Gleanntan Coming At Ya 18
Gleanntan Gee Whillikers **17**, 19
Gleanntan Gotixactlyrite 19
Gleanntan Grandxpose 19
Gloriette v Muencher Kindl 19

Go-to-ground events 22, 26, 91
Goodman, Mrs. Adele 15-16
Goodman, Walter 16-17
Grain-based feeds 52
Gray, John 10
Greyfriar's Bobby **10**
Grooming 24, 58, 60, 65
—equipment 59
Group competition 130-131
Guarding 147
Handler 127, 129
Health 42
—adult 95
—benefits of dog ownership 23
—insurance for pets 99
—journal 44
—puppy 30, 93
—senior dog 97, 124
Hearing 22
Heart disease 97
Heartworm 95, 115, **116, 117**
Heat cycle 102, 148
Heat-related problems 124
Hebrides islands 9
Heel 88-89
Helm, Brigitte **12**
Hepatitis 100-101
Hereditary health concerns 24
Here's Pandora of Morningsky **140**
Hermangiosarcoma 25
Heterodoxus spiniger **110**
High Times Gesture of Arreton 15
High Times kennels 15
High Times Miss Gesty 15, 16
Hip dysplasia 125
Hookworm **113**, 116
Homemade toys 40
House-training 36-37, 50, 73-74, 76-80
—puppy needs 74
—schedule 74, 80
Hunting 17, 22
Hypertrophic osteodystrophy 25
Hypothyroidism 25
Identification 67, 68
Independence 23-24
Infectious diseases 101
Insurance 99
Intelligence 23-24
Internal parasites 112-127
Introduction to Quarry 138
Iradell kennels 11, 13
Irritable aggression 146
Isle of Mull 9
Isle of Skye 9, 21
Isle of Skye kennels 20
Isle of Wight 9
Italy 20
Ivory Jock of Iradell 14
Ixodes dammini **107-108**
Jacinthe de Ricelaine 16, 17
Janisch, Frau 19
Jimmy de Ricelaine, 17
Jocelyn, Hon. Mrs. 11
Jojac's Rise and Shine 18
Judy, Will 22
Jumping up 78, 151
Junior Earthdog 138
Junior Showmanship 132
Kennel Club, The 26, 31
—address 139
Kidney problems 97
Koss, Michel 19
Lairdoglen Braveheart 19
Lairdoglen kennels 18
Lairdoglen Renaisance Man **20**
Lairdoglen Steel Magnolia **136**

Leanntan kennels 17
Leash 40, 81
—pulling on 89
Leave it 87, 148
Leptospirosis 100-101
Lifespan 97, 121
Little Cap of Stonebrae 15
Littlecreek Reay 21
Loneliness 142, 144, 151
Louse 110
Lucky Henry 12
Lyme disease 101
MacDonald, Jeanette 14
MacDonald, Lady 9
Malzeland kennels 12
Mammary cancer 102
Manville, Miss 12
Marking territory 146, 148
Master Earthdog 138
Maternal aggression 38
McCheane, Miss 10
Meat 52-53
Meerend kennels 12
Merrybrac kennels 11, 15
Merrybrac's Mustang 15
Merrymount kennels 11
Merrymount Sunset 11
Merrymount You'll Do 11, 14
Microchip 68
Miles, Lady Marcia 11
Milk 53
Miscellaneous Class 136
Mites 109, 110, 111
Montgomery County Kennel Club 17
Morningsky kennels 20
Morris and Essex show 14
Mosquitoes 111, 115, 117
Mounting 102, 146, 149
Nail clipping 60, 63, 65
Nail-grinder 65
Name 83, 88
National History Museum 13
National Obedience Champion 134
Netherlands 20-21
Neutering 35, 95, 102, 146, 148
Nipping 49
Non-core vaccines 101
Norway 20
Obedience 85
—classes 24, 90
—competition 24
—Trial Champion 134
—trials 90, 132
Obee, Lia 20
Obesity 58, 126
Of Mynd kennels 12
Off 78, 152
Okay 85, 89, 153
Old-dog syndrome 123
Olivia kennels 18
Olivia Wild West 21
Opulous of Skyeline 20
Origin of breed 9
Original purpose 22, 26
Orthopedic problems
—senior dog 125
Osteochondritis dissecans 125
Other dogs 102, 148
Other pets 72
Otodectes cynotis 109
Outdoor safety 42, 151
Ovariohysterectomy 102
Ownership 31, 33-34
—expenses of 42
—health benefits of 23
Pack animals 48, 82
Paper-training 74, 79
Parainfluenza 100-101
Parasites
—control 95

—external 104-111
—internal 112-117
Parent club 132
Parting the coat 60
Parvovirus 100-101
Patience 72, 81
Personality 22
Pesare, Michael 19
Plants 45, 98
Playtime 87
Pless, Princess 19
Poisons 42, 44-45, 98
Poland 20
Popularity 9
Positive reinforcement 45, 80-81, 83, 91, 147
Possessive behavior 147
Practicing 80, 86
—commands 84
Praise 71, 80-81, 90, 152
Preventive care 93, 95, 97
Professional help 86, 150
Proglottid 115
Prostate problems 102
Punishment 51, 80-81, 147
Puppy
—appearance 31
—coat 59
—common problems 49
—diet 52
—dominance games 147
—establishing leadership 71
—feeding 52
—first car ride 46
—first night in new home 45
—grooming 59
—health 30, 93
—kindergarten training 82
—limp 25
—meeting the family 44
—needs 74
—personality 33, 95
—proofing 41, 45
—selection 31, 33, 70, 93
—show quality 33, 127-128
—socialization 46
—supplies for 35
—teething 41, 50
—training 48, 70, 81
Pyne, Mrs. Eben W. 15
Quetzan Brucie O'Duff 18
Quiet 153
Quizas Casey O'Bruce 18, **19**
Quizas kennels 18
Rabies 100-101
Rally obedience 134
Rawhide 38
Rewards 71, 80, 81, 89
—food 81
Rhabditis 116
Rhosneigr kennels 11
Rhosneigr Red Shoes 11
Rhosneigr Rising Star 11
Roaming 102
Roblyn A Chorus Line **19**
Roblyn kennels 18
Roblyn's Bhain Inghean, 18
Roblyn's Hotter Than That 18
Roblyn's Racy Rachel, 18
Rohrich, Roxanna 19
Romach 12
Rope toys 39
Roundworm **112**, 113, **116**
Routine 50, 72
Rover Run kennels 18
Rover Run The California Zephyr 18
Royalist of Merrymount 11
Russia 20
Safety 36, 41, 44-45, 76, 78, 87, 149
—commands 87

—in the car 87
—outdoors 42, 151
—yard 151
Sand Island Sam Fifield **15**
Sand Island Soltaire **16**
Sanderson, William 12
Sarcoptes scabiei **109**
Scabies 109
Scandinavia 20
Scent attraction 79
Schedule 50, 72, 74
Scottish Chief of Arreton 13
Scottish Terrier 9, 22-23
Seamist Joyful Noise **139**
Senior dog 97
—behavioral changes 122
—dental care 126
—diet 56, 125
—exercise 126
—health 97
—signs of aging 121
—veterinary care 124
Senior Earthdog 138
Sensitivity 23
Separation anxiety 141-142, 144
Sex differences 35, 146, 148
Show quality 33, 127, 128
Shows
—costs of 128
Simonds, Carol and Janice 18
Sit 83, 152
Sit/stay 85
Size 22
Skye limp 25
Skye Terrier Club of America 15, 17
Skyeline kennels 20
Skylab kennels 20
Skyroyal kennels 20
Smid, Olga 18, 20
Smith, Gail 19
Sniffing 148
Socialization 46, 48, 82, 95, 145, 148
Soft toys 39
Spanish Armada 9
Spanish white dogs 9
Spaying 95, 102, 148
Specialty show 132
Spinnrock, Elke 20
Spleen 25
Sporting dogs 91
Spot bath 60
Stay 85, 89
Stealing food 155
Steinbacher, Herr 19
Stevenson, Robert Louis 14
Stillman, Michael 13
Stonebrae kennels 15
Stormy Weather **14**
Stress 85
Submission 145
Supervision 49-50, 78
Surgery 102
Sweden 20
Swensen, Mr. and Mrs. 20
Switzerland 20
Table scraps 53
Taenia pisiformis **115**
Talisker kennels 19
Tapeworm 114, **115**, **116**
Teeth 22, 95, 98
Teething 41
—period 50, 149
Temperament 22, 38
—evaluation 95
Terrier instincts 22, 24
Territorial aggression 146
Territory marking 148
Testicular cancer 102
Therapy dog 91
Thirst 57

Tick-borne diseases 107
Ticks **107-108**
Timing 79, 81, 87
Toby of Iradell 14
Tompkins, Mrs. W. H. 15
Toxascaris leonine 112
Toxins 42, 44-45, 53, 98
Toxocara canis **112**
Toys 38-39, 41, 51, 76, 78, 149
Tracheobronchitis 100
Tracking 91, 132, 134
Tracking Dog 134
Tracking Dog Excellent 134
Training 23-24, 49-50
—basic principles 70, 81
—clicker 91
—consistency in 47
—crate 37, 79
—early 48
—getting started 81
—importance of timing 79, 87
—practice 80
—proper attitude 73
—tips 49
Traveling 36, 46, 87
Treats 45, 55, 71, 81
—weaning off in training 89
Trichuris sp. **114**
Tricks 91
Tug-of-war 147
Tuukan kennels 20
Type 127-128
United Kennel Club 140
—address 139
United Kingdom 9
United States 132
United States Dog Agility Association 137
Urine marking 102
Utility Dog 133
Utility Dog Excellent 134
Vaccinations 44, 47, 95, 101
—core vs. non-core 101
Variable Surface Tracking 134
Ventre, Patie 139
Veterinarian 34, 38-39, 42, 87, 95, 98, 141
—selection of 97
Veterinary insurance 99
Veterinary specialties 99
Victoria, Queen 9
Visiting the litter 33
Vitamin A toxicity 53
Voice 73
Wait 87
Walker, Mrs. Helen Whitehouse 132
Water 56, 76
—bowls 35
—excessive intake 57
Wattie 11
Weber, Laura 18
Weehunt, Edrie 17
West Highland White Terrier 22
West Nile virus 111
Westerholm, Mrs. Hjordis 20
Westminster Kennel Club 13, 129
Whining 45, 51, 77
Whipworm **114**
Winter dogs 21
Wishau of Iradell 18
Wolverley Chummie 10, **11**, **13**
Wolverley Duchess 10
Wolverley Jock 10
Wolverley kennels 10, 11
Wolverley Roy 10
Working ability 22
Working trials 132
World Canine Freestyle Organization 139
World Wars 10, 11, 13, 15
Worm control 114
Yard 42, 151
Yugoslavia 20

My Skye Terrier

PUT YOUR PUPPY'S FIRST PICTURE HERE

Dog's Name _____

Date _____ Photographer _____